CLASSIC
CATERPILLAR
CRAWLERS

Caterpillar

KEITH HADDOCK & ERIC C. ORLEMANN

MBI Publishing Company

First published in 2001 by MBI Publishing Company, 380 Jackson Street, Suite 200, St. Paul, MN 55101-3885 USA

MBI Publishing Company books are also available at discounts in bulk quantity for industrial or sales-promotional use. For details write to Special Sales Manager at Motorbooks International Wholesalers & Distributors, 380 Jackson Street, Suite 200, St. Paul, MN 55101-3885 USA

Library of Congress Cataloging-in-Publication Data Available
ISBN 0-7603-0917-5

Designed by Katie Sonmor
Edited by Paul Johnson

Printed in China

On the front cover: In 1933, the Diesel Seventy-Five was Caterpillar's most powerful offerings. The Cat D11000 diesel engine installed in the big tractor produced 83 drawbar and 98 belt horsepower. This vintage 1934 model Diesel Seventy-Five is tractor serial number 2E452. Owner: Tyler family. *ECO*

On the frontispiece: The Thirty's distinctive has made it a collector's favorite around the world. Although it is not as large as the Sixty, many superb restored examples exist today. This narrow-gauge, tailseat Caterpillar Thirty is a 1929 San Leandro built machine, carrying serial number S8099. Owner: Ron Miller. *ECO*

On the title page: By early 1932, the Diesel Sixty was marketed as the Caterpillar Diesel, though most in the industry simply referred to it as the Diesel Sixty-Five. It was powered by the Cat D9900 diesel engine, rated at 68 drawbar, 79 belt , and 85 brake horsepower. Owners: Ted Halton of The Halton Co. and Dave Smith. *ECO*

On the back cover, top: This Best 110 hp Traction Engine, often referred to as a "steamer," is a 1906 vintage machine No. 175. Equipped with the wider drive-wheel option, it is one of only a couple of Best steam tractors in fully restored operable condition today. Owner: Joseph A. Heidrick, Sr. Foundation. *ECO* **Bottom:** The D2 model line was the smallest diesel powered crawler tractor to be manufactured by Caterpillar. First introduced in 1938 in the 3J-series (40-inch gauge), and the 5J-series (50-inch gauge), it was an instant hit with farmers. It was small enough to work between orchard rows, as well as large enough for open field disking and plowing duties. Owner: Tom Novak. *ECO*

CONTENTS

ACKNOWLEDGMENTS

I would like to thank the following individuals who have provided information, and given me the support I needed to complete this book on Caterpillar. Jim Serink, Finning Ltd., Edmonton, Alberta; Steve Sager, Hawthorne Machinery Company, San Diego, California; Ray Hooley, Lincoln, England.

And of course a big thankyou to my wife, Barbara, who has supported this project with many hours of dedicated editing, and provided much useful advice on its presentation. Her grammatical expertise and literary experience have transformed my original text into a very readable story.

— Keith Haddock

Books such as this one require a year or two of advanced planning and research to make them a reality. While working on my *Caterpillar Chronicle* book project, which was published in 2000 by MBI, I was simultaneously preparing research and photography that would be utilized in this co-authored endeavor. Early on, it was clear that there were just too many "classic" Caterpillar crawler tractor variations that would have to be edited out of the "Chronicle" project because of lack of space. Not wanting the research and additional photography to go to waste, Motorbooks International decided that the early Caterpillar crawlers, along with their Holt and Best predecessors, needed to be revisited one more time, in a more detailed and expanded fashion. Working in conjunction with my good friend and fellow author, Keith Haddock, this book came to be.

I would like to express my sincerest thanks to Caterpillar, Inc., for the interest and cooperation they have given me over the years in helping me make these projects a reality. I would also like to acknowledge Jeff Hawkinson, Lea McCall, and Nicole L. Thaxton for their additional help and guidance over the months and years with Caterpillar.

I would also like to extend my appreciation to the many individual Caterpillar tractor owners and operators who have so graciously allowed me access to their prized machines and collections. Thanks to Lorry Dunning and the Joseph A. Heidrick, Sr. Foundation, Ed Akin, Doug Veerkamp, Keith Clark, Ted Halton, Dave Smith, Brent Smith, Marv Fery, Paul Kirsch, Don Dougherty, George E. Logue, Tom Novak, Kent Bates, Larry Maasdam, Ron Miller, Allen F. Anderson, Paul Tyler, Mike Tyler, Howard Bowers, Peter M. Holt, Charles Bogar, Patrick J. Eder, Dan Plote, Bob LaVoie, and Thomas Berry of the Historical Construction Equipment Association.

For individuals looking to find additional information and others like themselves who enjoy all things "CAT," the Antique Caterpillar Machinery Owners Club might be a good place to start. Officially recognized by Caterpillar, Inc., the club brings lovers of early Caterpillar, as well as Holt and Best, equipment together to share information and stories, as well as maintenance and restoration tips and advice. For further information, contact:

Antique Caterpillar Machinery Owners Club (ACMOC)
P.O Box 2220
East Peoria, IL 61611
www.acmoc.org

— Eric C. Orlemann

INTRODUCTION

Welcome to the ultimate book on Caterpillar crawler tractors, containing brand new photography, many new stories, and a lot of in-depth, never-before-published information on Caterpillar's agricultural machinery. By combining Eric Orlemann's recent detailed research at Caterpillar Inc.'s corporate offices with the valuable resource of my Caterpillar literature collection, amassed over a 40-year period, I have been able to write a very accurate account of Caterpillar's crawler tractors. Much of the information originated from corporate correspondence and sales data. My text, combined with Eric Orlemann's brilliant and imaginative photography, results in a book I hope you will enjoy and want to keep for a lifetime.

This book is a detailed history of Caterpillar's crawler tractors. It is not intended to cover details of other Caterpillar products although they are mentioned where appropriate. The book focuses on Caterpillar Tractor Company's history, and crawler tractor development from its origin to 1955, the year the famous D9 tractor was introduced. From that time the company's products grew dramatically larger, and its product base broadened to include equipment for heavy construction, mining, logging, and many other industries, as well as its traditional agricultural equipment. It was not possible in a book of this size to cover all these products, but the final chapter briefly covers Caterpillar's rapid expansion since 1955, and shows how the company's name is not only synonymous with crawler tractors, but a whole host of other equipment types as well.

Tractor horsepower figures stated throughout this book are those quoted in Caterpillar's own specification sheets and may differ from other published data. Since 1920, all makes of tractors have been tested at the Agricultural Engineering Department of the University of Nebraska in Lincoln under the Nebraska Test Law in that state. Over the years these tests have become known as the Nebraska Tractor Tests and are a useful reference for comparing the performance of different makes of tractors. Because the results of these tests were subject to varying factors such as temperature, barometric pressure, type of fuel, and how the tractor was set up, different results were sometimes reported for the same tractor. And these results often differed from the manufacturer's published data. To avoid any confusion this book therefore relies solely on the manufacturer's data.

— *Keith Haddock*

CHAPTER ONE

HOLT AND BEST

Caterpillar did not enter the world as a startup company, with an idea for a product and some funding to start building it. Instead, the company's history encompasses two separate and successful manufacturers who entered the tractor business in its infancy. Both men had the determination and ability to build a quality product, and their innovations would encourage one another and help solidify the tractor's essential role in agriculture. Decades later, the two companies would merge to form one of the world's premiere heavy equipment firms. But in the beginning, these two manufacturers started business as competitors.

ORIGINS OF HOLT AND BEST

By the late 1880s, California's gold rush was almost over, but its fertile farmlands continued to promise rich yields. Teams of men, horses, and mules toiled for long hours to plow, plant, and harvest vast fields of wheat. Yet California's farmers knew that laboring by hand was an ineffective way to extract the land's bounty. They needed mechanization—machines to complete the work faster and more efficiently than the traditional horse and mule teams.

The farmers' needs provided just the right opportunity for two inventive individuals who had moved out west to make their fortunes. Benjamin Holt and Daniel Best were destined to revolutionize agriculture and to change road building forever. They would become the predecessors of the Caterpillar Tractor Company.

HOLT 75
Originally introduced in 1913, the Holt 75 model line was a real workhorse for the company. This restored Stockton-produced Holt 75 (Model T-8), No. 3564, is a 1918 vintage tractor and is powered by a Holt-built M-7 four-cylinder 7-1/2x8-inch bore-and-stroke, valve-in-head gas motor. Owner: Joseph A. Heidrick, Sr. Foundation. *ECO*

BEST 110-HORSEPOWER TRACTION ENGINE

Big and imposing, the Best Traction Engine, along with its Holt counterparts, ushered in mobile steam-power in the western United States, marking the beginning of the end of "animal-power" in the fields. *ECO*

BEST 110-HORSEPOWER TRACTION ENGINE

This Best 110-horsepower Traction Engine, often referred to as a "steamer," is a 1906 vintage machine No. 175. Equipped with the wider drive-wheel option, it is one of only a couple of Best steam tractors in fully restored operable condition today. There are approximately 12 or so of these Best behemoths still in existence in various states of disrepair or restoration. Sadly, none of the Holt Road Engines are known to exist. Owner: Joseph A. Heidrick, Sr. Foundation. *ECO*

EARLY HOLT ACTIVITIES

Benjamin Holt was born in Loudon, New Hampshire, on January 1, 1849, the seventh of eight children. He began his career by joining his father in the family lumber business in nearby Concord. In 1865, Benjamin's brother, Charles, immigrated to California, and established C.H. Holt & Company in San Francisco. There, he sold hardwoods from his father's company to local wagon and boat builders. Unfortunately, wood seasoned in the damp New Hampshire climate shrank, warped, and dried out in the hot, dry California air. The Holts tried seasoning the wood

in San Francisco, but since this was also often cool and damp, there was little difference.

To solve this problem, Charles looked farther inland for a warmer, drier climate, and decided to set up a wheel company in the town of Stockton, some 80 miles east. In 1883 younger brother Benjamin Holt journeyed across the country on the recently completed transcontinental railroad to head up the new Stockton Wheel Company. Stockton's dry climate proved perfect for seasoning wood, and its location was an excellent choice because it had good river connections with San Francisco to the west, wagon routes to the mines in the east, and was close to the fertile San Joaquin Valley.

Always eager for something new, the Holt brothers tried building railroad cars and streetcars, but soon abandoned this unprofitable idea. They gradually extended their facilities to make possible the manufacture of large items such as steamboat boilers, mining cars and wagons, and farm machinery. The factory soon comprised many departments, including Benjamin's important experimental shop. But they also sold lumber, chains, belting, and many other small hardware items. By 1900 the factory buildings took up an impressive eight blocks, and switching yards provided access to two railroads.

But the vast acres of the San Joaquin Valley wheat fields provided the ambitious and inventive Holt brothers with a huge and lucrative agricultural market, and their always-innovative products firmly established the Holt name in the farm machinery business. After only two years in Stockton, they bought several combine patents, expanded their factory, and put their first combined harvester on the market in 1886. "The Holt Bros. Improved Link Belt Combined Harvester" featured linked chains and sprockets instead of the usual belt-driven pulleys, and was pulled by 18 horses.

Benjamin studied the early combines as they worked in the fields and realized that the dust caused the tight gears to wear quickly, creating more friction, which meant even more horses were needed to haul the machines. The gears also clanked and growled, frightening the horses. Runaway teams were a problem, and horses were often injured or killed. Benjamin Holt designed his first machines with link belts instead of tight gears, and they were advertised as being very quiet.

Benjamin's interest then turned to the traction engine, and in 1890 he introduced a steam-traction engine of his own design. Nicknamed "Old Betsy," this machine was the first of its time to feature steering clutches. In 1893, Ben earned a patent for his innovation of disengaging the power to one driving wheel or the other to aid steering.

In 1892 the brothers changed the company name from the Stockton Wheel Company to the Holt

HOLT TRACKED ROAD ENGINE
Shown in March 1905 is the Holt Tracked Road Engine, originally built out of a round-wheel Holt Road Engine No. 77. This prototype, which was first tested on November 24, 1904, was photographed by company photographer Charles Clements. He is credited with giving the company the "Caterpillar" name after seeing Benjamin Holt's tractor creation working in the field, and exclaiming, "If that don't look like a monster caterpillar!" *Courtesy Caterpillar, Inc. Corporate Archives*

Manufacturing Company to better reflect the ever-expanding range of products it developed and manufactured. Benjamin Holt, now the company's president, was in charge of everything.

DANIEL BEST'S EARLY ACTIVITIES

Daniel Best's career, meanwhile, took a much more circuitous path. Instead of becoming involved in his own family's lumber business, he tried his hand at many jobs in various locations. In his teens he did work for a while in his father's sawmill in Iowa. Then at the age of 20, attracted by the lure of greater opportunities, and of course gold, he decided to head west to make his fortune. First he went to Washington, and since he had experience, took a job in a lumber mill in Steptoville (now Walla Walla). Next he had a brief try at running his own mill, and when this proved unprofitable, Best moved on to Portland, Oregon. There he once again found work in a lumber mill, but soon tired of it, and invested with a partner in a south Washington gold mine. Best did have some successful strikes, but unluckily

HOLT TRACKED ROAD ENGINE
This detail view of the Holt Tracked Road Engine from March 1905 shows how the track assembly was crudely attached to the modified steamer No. 77 chassis. It was the first of approximately seven modified design configurations that were fitted to three tractors. The third tractor, Holt No. 111, was equipped with the seventh track design and was to become the first such unit sold to a paying customer. It was referred to as the "Holt Brothers Paddle Wheel Improved Traction Engine." *ECO Collection*

HOLT 40
The first gasoline engine–powered tracked tractor sold by Holt to a paying customer was its No. 1003 Model 40, in 1908. Even though two tractors preceded this unit (the first tested in December 1906), they were never sold into private service. Pictured is No. 1003 at the Holt Stockton facilities in September, just before its final delivery. *Courtesy Caterpillar, Inc. Corporate Archives*

for him, his raft capsized in the Snake River, causing him to lose all his gold and almost his life.

Between the years 1862 and 1869, Daniel Best continued his search for a fulfilling and profitable career. He worked a series of mining and lumbering jobs, and finally ended up in Marysville, California, where he started work on his brother Henry's ranch. After the harvest, Best observed all the farmers transporting their grain to town to be cleaned. He envisioned how convenient it would be if a portable cleaner could be brought in to clean the grain right in the field. This brainwave would prove very profitable for him in the future.

He spent that winter designing and building just such an invention. By next year's harvest, Best was ready to begin testing his portable cleaner machine. It was a great success, and the design earned him his first patent in April 1871. Best continued with his farming inventions, but was always on the lookout for more profitable endeavors. In 1874 he had another attempt at gold mining, and in 1877 he received another patent for an improved washing machine. But by 1880, Best was back on the farm designing

progressively bigger harvesters, demanded by the California farmers.

With his business expanding, Best moved to San Leandro, California. He named his new operation Daniel Best Agricultural Works, a company that would provide stiff competition for Holt. Indeed, the two companies became fierce rivals, vying for control of the farm machinery business in the west. Best soon noticed that farmers were attaching his grain cleaners to combine harvesters. He responded by producing his first combine in 1885. Best's career was now firmly entrenched in manufacturing.

To meet the farmers' needs for bigger machines, the combine harvesters built by Best, Holt, and other manufacturers were becoming so heavy that horse teams could hardly haul them through the fields. The inventors plainly saw that a better source of power than horses was needed to propel the huge combines. Horses needed expensive, year-round upkeep, yet they produced money for the farmer chiefly during spring plowing and harvest periods. The big teams were hard to control, and horses often died of sunstroke or exhaustion in the hot, dry, dusty conditions. Manufacturers

needed to address this problem, and steam-traction engines seemed the only viable solution. Both Daniel Best and Benjamin Holt were eager to conquer this new market, and their inventions would signal the end of large horse teams and the dawn of mechanized, high production farming.

In the spring of 1888, in San Leandro, Best saw a demonstration of a steam-traction engine designed by a blacksmith named Marquis de Lafayette Remington. Best was thoroughly impressed with Remington's "Rough and Ready" traction engine. He immediately bought the rights to build the 30-horsepower machine to sell on the West Coast, agreeing not to market it in Remington's home state of Oregon. Best set to work right away to produce traction engine power for his combine harvesters, and on February 8, 1889, the very first Best traction engine was ready for shipping. Best's engines were very innovative in design, featuring vertical boilers and only one front wheel. They weighed 11 tons. The first four Best steamers went to work in the Sacramento Valley in 1889, and reputedly moved twice as fast as horses.

Holt's first traction engine, "Betsy," appeared shortly after in 1890, the first in a series of 130 wheel-type steamers

that he would produce over the next 24 years. Betsy eventually became the plant mascot, used to move machinery and loaded rail cars. Many new operators also learned their skills on this machine.

In the last decade of the nineteenth century, both Holt and Best offered steam-traction engines, commonly known as "steamers," to match up with their own combines. Successful models for Holt included the 40-horsepower Junior Road Engine from 1891, the 60-horsepower Standard Road Engine from 1895, and the powerful 70-horsepower Senior Road Engine. Best's popular models included the 50-horsepower Traction Engine from 1889 and the 110-horsepower model from 1897. While the Holt and Best model lines were almost identical, customers clearly favored the Best steamers in the field because their engines were more powerful. But when it came to combines, the Holt machines took the lead. By 1912, Best had sold some 1,351 steam combines, and Holt had sold around 8,000.

The Holt and Best steam-traction engines were very successful on dry, stable ground, but on the soft, soggy peat soil of the San Joaquin River Delta area, the tremendously

carry children in city parks. In 1770, Richard L. Edgeworth of England applied steam power to a crawler-type vehicle, and in 1825 another Englishman, Sir George Cayley, received a patent for "a crawler apparatus that placed an endless chain belt over the two wheels on each side of a wagon." In 1832 a British textile manufacturer, John Heathcote, built a 30-ton steam-plowing engine. It apparently worked well, but during a trial, it sank out of sight into a deep swamp. Heathcote didn't have the financial support to continue the venture.

Lack of funding was the common cause of failure for several other individuals who built and tried to market versions of the crawler track principle. These included Warren P. Miller of Maysville, California, who demonstrated his track-type steam plow at the State Fair in 1858; George Minnis, whose steam-plowing engine on tracks was praised by the U.S. Department of Agriculture in their 1869 report; and R. C. Parvin of Philadelphia, Pennsylvania, who demonstrated his crawler engine at the Illinois State Fair in 1871. Although all these designs appeared promising at the time, none reached beyond the prototype stage, and none were sold commercially.

Alvin O. Lombard of Maine is credited with developing and building America's first successful crawler tractor. Designed for hauling logs in the winter, the machine resembled a railroad locomotive driven by crawler tracks instead of wheels, while the front end rested on a sled with runners to aid steering in snow. The prototype was tested in 1900, and after some redesign, three more steam crawlers were built in 1901 and 1902. The first machine sold to a paying customer went to a logger in Waterville, Maine, in 1903. With much publicity, the Lombard crawler engines became popular in the eastern United States with 205 recorded sales up to 1915. The Phoenix Manufacturing Company of Eau Claire built some 65 of these under license.

Benjamin Holt had heard about the crawler machines, and took a tour of the United States and Europe to learn exactly what had been accomplished with crawler tracks. This research convinced him that crawlers were the answer to the flotation and traction problems with wheel tractors. He watched the Lombard tractors in operation, and soon afterward instructed his mechanics to remove the rear wheels on the 40-horsepower steam-driven Holt Junior Road Engine (serial No. 77), and replace them with a pair

heavy steamers would easily mire down in the fields. To provide better flotation, both Holt and Best increased the wheel diameters to the largest practical size. Then they increased the wheel widths and fitted extension wheels on the outer rims of the regular wheels. This made the tractors extremely wide—some to ridiculous proportions. The whole idea was to increase flotation by reducing ground pressure, but the tractors, some up to 46 feet wide, went beyond practical limitations. The wide wheels and their supporting structure added weight to the machines and made them more difficult to maneuver. And the tractors had to be taken apart when moving to a new location. To solve the problem, the manufacturers needed another technological breakthrough, which arrived with the invention of the belted crawler track.

THE FIRST "CATERPILLAR" TRACTOR ARRIVES

The crawler track was something that inventors had dreamed about and experimented with for decades. The precise origin of the crawler track principle is obscured in history, but we know that Frenchman M. D'Hermand designed a crawler-tread trailer pulled by goats in 1713 to

NORTHERN HOLT 45B
Only four examples of the two front-wheel-steering Holt 45B gas-engined tractors were ever built—two by the Northern Holt Company of Minneapolis, Minnesota, and two by The Canadian Holt Company, Ltd., all in 1909. Pictured in 1911 at the Peoria plant in Illinois is one of the original Minneapolis-built machines. Today, only one example of this unique Holt tractor (No. 102) is in existence, and is currently part of the Fred C. Heidrick Ag History Center, located in Woodland, California. *ECO Collection*

of tracks 9 feet long and 2 feet wide. Thus, the first Holt crawler tractor was born. On its first field test on November 24, 1904, it reportedly performed with complete satisfaction. Alvin Lombard maintained for the rest of his life that Holt simply copied his invention without making a cash settlement or paying royalties.

Several inventors in England were also simultaneously developing the crawler track. David Roberts, chief engineer with R. Hornsby & Sons of Grantham, patented a crawler track design in 1904. The following year, a Roberts "chain track" was fitted to a Hornsby oil tractor built in 1896. Several Hornsby steam-and-oil-powered tractors were completed with crawler tracks. But despite much promotion, including the first film ever made for commercial purposes (1908), and demonstrations for high-ranking military personnel, the idea did not catch on.

Having received only one civilian order for a tracked tractor, to be used in northern Canada for hauling coal, the Hornsby company became disillusioned and in 1914 sold the patent rights of the "chain track" to Holt Manufacturing

HOLT 60
The Holt 60 was originally introduced in 1911. It was built at the Stockton plant as the Holt 60 (Model T-7), and at the Peoria facilities as the Holt 40-60 (Model T-4). Pictured is a 1911 Stockton-built T-7 machine, powered by a four-cylinder Holt M-6, 7x8-inch bore-and-stroke, valve-in-head gas motor. The Peoria-built tractors utilized a Holt M-3 gas motor with an "Ell-head" valve design, though the engine was the same size as the Stockton model. *Courtesy Caterpillar, Inc. Corporate Archives*

HOLT 75
Pictured is a 1917 Holt 75 (Model T-8) produced in Peoria, Illinois. Built primarily for military duties, it differed from the Stockton-built tractors in the design of its crawler assemblies and its cooling system, though both utilized the same M-7 gas motor. All Peoria-built T-8 tractors were of this configuration. Production would end on this design in late 1918. *ECO Collection*

for $8,000. Ironically, the crawler tractor gave Winston Churchill the idea of building the tank when the British Army needed a new fighting machine in World War I. Designers had to start from scratch to construct a suitable track-laying machine, when just a year earlier, Hornsby had sold what they needed to Holt. And just to add further to the irony, when the British army needed crawler tractors for the war effort in 1914, it purchased them from Holt!

The term "Caterpillar" was first used to refer to a Holt machine in March 1905. Benjamin and his nephew, Pliny Holt, took the regular Holt photographer, Charles Clements, out to their ranch near Stockton to photograph the very first Holt crawler tractor in operation. The Holts referred to this machine as a "platform wheel engine." When Clements arrived at the ranch, he expected to see a tractor with the usual large driving wheels, but was amazed when he saw the new form of propulsion. He exclaimed in awe, "If that don't look like a monster caterpillar." After developing his images, Clements marked the first set of negatives "Caterpillar." The name was soon

adopted as Holt's trademark, and was registered as such with the U.S. Patent Office in 1910.

HOLT GASOLINE TILLER-WHEEL TRACTORS

The first crawler tractors were based on steam-powered traction engines because that was the most common motive power available at the time. However, while Benjamin Holt was busy developing and testing his steam tractors, he kept a watchful eye on another type of motive power unfolding at the same time—the gasoline engine. With the idea of further developing gasoline engine technology, Holt, along with nephew Pliny, established the Aurora Engine Company at Stockton in October 1906. They made fast progress, and by December 1906, a prototype tractor with a gasoline engine was ready for testing. A second test machine was built in early 1908, and later that same year, Holt sold the first "Caterpillar" gasoline crawler tractor to a paying customer. It was designated the Model 40, and given serial No. 1003. Power came from a four-cylinder, 6x8-inch bore-and-stroke, valve-in-head engine rated at 25-drawbar horsepower.

17

HOLT 75
The last version of the Holt 75 (Model T-8) to be produced was the "4000" serial number series. Produced from 1921 to 1924, it was only built in Stockton, and all were painted in a light shade of green. New to this model line were redesigned radiator and crawler assemblies. Pictured in 1999 is a 1921 vintage model No. 4008. In all, there were only 67 of this type ever built. Owner: Larry Maasdam. *ECO*

Compactness was not an attribute of these early crawler tractors. The long frame supported the large-diameter steering clutches and brakes at the rear and the bulky engine and radiator at the front. In between, an array of open mechanical contrivances made up of gears, wheels, shafts, and linkages helped to propel the clanking iron mass. At the front a "tiller" wheel helped to steer the machine and provided support for the long frame. Steering was accomplished by cranking the steering wheel, which drove through a worm onto the tiller-wheel support frame. But the steering wheel was not effective for anything more than minor directional changes unless one of the crawlers was disengaged by its respective clutch, and then braked for a tighter turn. The tiller wheel could be turned almost 90 degrees to the frame, so that a very tight turn could be accomplished if one track was locked. The operator sat on the side of the tractor where he could oversee the work

going on behind, and at the same time keep a visual check on the open mechanisms to make sure everything was working properly. About 56 of the Model 40 tractors were made at the Stockton factory until 1909.

The success of the Holt 40 gave the Holts the impetus they needed to expand the crawler tractor business. First they upgraded the 40 to the 45-series, which commenced production at the Stockton plant in 1909. The 45-series was similar in appearance to the 40 model, except it was powered by a different engine, the Holt M-1 valve-in-head gas engine with a 6-1/2x8-inch bore and stroke. Then the Holts looked to expand their manufacturing base. They saw the Midwest as having the greatest potential for agriculture mechanization. Accordingly, the Northern Holt Company was incorporated in March 1909, in Minneapolis, Minnesota. Pliny Holt was president and his brother, Ben C. Holt, was vice-president. Pliny Holt was

HOLT 120

The largest tractor produced by Holt was its "120." The Holt 120 started testing in 1914 as the Model A-PEP equipped with a Holt-built six-cylinder 7-1/2x8-inch bore-and-stroke "enclosed" Peoria motor. When production officially started in 1915, it would be equipped with the Holt M-8 gas engine with the "Ell-head" valve design, and be known as the Model T-9. All other specifications of the engine would remain unchanged. The Holt 120 (Model T-9) shown is a 1917 version built in Peoria. All Holt 120 tractors were produced in Peoria, and shared the same crawler and radiator designs found on the Holt 75 also being built at the same facilities. Only one complete Holt 120 is known to have survived today, and it is part of the Fred C. Heidrick Ag History Center in Woodland, California. *ECO Collection*

familiar with the city because he had studied engineering there at the University of Minnesota. Parts for the tractors were shipped from Stockton to Minneapolis for assembly by the Diamond Iron Works under a contract signed in May 1909. At the same time, Pliny Holt was eyeing Canada as another huge market for his tractors, and made a trip to Winnipeg, Manitoba, to explore farm machinery business operations in Canada. The Canadian Holt Company Ltd. was established in 1909 at Winnipeg, with all Canadian rights to be owned by the Northern Holt Company.

But the Northern Holt Company ventures did not work out as expected. In the firmer soils in these regions, the crawler tractors did not provide as much advantage over wheeled machines—at least not enough advantage to justify

their higher cost. A Holt crawler sold for $4,000, whereas a Hart-Parr wheel tractor of similar horsepower could be purchased for $2,650. Another problem was a severe cash shortage. It would have taken huge sums of capital to purchase and equip the factories that Holt envisioned. In any event, Northern Holt failed after only two tractors had sold from each location. These were known as the 45B models, and differed from the Stockton-built machines in that they had two front wheels for steering instead of the usual tiller wheel.

The Holt brothers did not give up with the disappointing failure of Northern Holt. They were still convinced that expansion to the east was imperative. Pliny Holt heard of another facility just east of Peoria, Illinois, that might be suitable for his company's needs. The premises were in the

HOLT 18 MIDGET
Introduced in 1914, the Holt 18 "Midget" was the smallest tiller-wheeled tractor built by the company. The engine in the Midget was a Holt-designed four-cylinder 4-1/2x5-1/2-inch bore-and-stroke "Ell-head" motor. Last year of production for the little tractor was 1917. Total production for the Midget amounted to 347 tractors, all built at the Stockton facilities. *ECO Collection*

process of being vacated by their former owners, who were in bankruptcy proceedings. On inspection, Holt found it to be a relatively modern plant, ideally located, and perfect for what he had in mind. So a deal was finalized on October 25, 1909, that would make Peoria the company's new headquarters. The following year, the name "Caterpillar" was registered as the company's official trademark.

Tractor production got under way immediately at Holt's newly acquired plant. The first tractor was shipped from Peoria in 1910. It was a Holt 45-series, the same tractor that had been started back at Stockton the previous year. However, the Peoria model was known as the 30-45 (T-1). Ninety-four Holt 45s were built up to 1913 at the Peoria plant, while another 154 were built at Stockton up to 1911. In addition, 72 Holt 40 (T-2 series) tractors were built at Peoria in 1913. They differed from the Stockton-built machines in that they were powered by a four-cylinder, M-2 gasoline engine with a 7x8-inch bore and stroke.

In 1911, Holt brought out a larger tiller-wheel tractor, the model 60-series, which was built in both the company's plants. The Stockton machine was designated the T-7 with a four-cylinder Holt M-6, 7x8-inch bore-and-stroke, valve-in-head gas engine. Those built in Peoria were referred to as the 40-60 (T-4) tractors. They were basically the same machine, except that the T-4 was equipped with a Holt M-3 gas engine of the same size, and featured an "Ell-head" valve design.

Sales were quite encouraging on the Holt 60 tractors until their manufacturing life was brought to a close during World War I. The company sold 691 units of the Stockton T-7 version before production ceased in 1915, while the Peoria T-4 managed a respectable 260 units sold up to 1916. Some 63 of the Holt 60 tractors went for military purposes.

The most popular of all the Holt tiller-wheel tractors was the 75, and it turned out to be the most famous too. With a production run lasting up to 1924, it was the last tiller-wheel tractor made by either Holt or Best. This heavyweight was first produced at the Stockton plant in 1913, when it was known as the Holt 60-75 (A-NVS). It was powered by a four-cylinder Holt M-7, 7-1/2x8-inch bore-and-stroke, valve-in-head gas engine. Peoria joined in with the Holt 75 manufacture in 1914 when a special run of tractors equipped with a Holt M-5 engine incorporating an "Ell-head" valve layout began. This design, the T-6 series, was not particularly successful, and the model was withdrawn the following year after only 16 had been built. In 1915 the Peoria plant commenced production of the same 75 model already being built at Stockton, but by this time tractors from both plants were known as the Holt 75 (T-8) model.

Up to 1918 most of the Holt 75 tractors shipped from the Peoria plant were destined for the war effort in Europe. In addition, records show that 442 Holt 75s were built at the Lincoln, England, plant of Ruston & Hornsby Ltd. in

1917 and 1918. The Peoria-built Holt 75 military version carried the same engine, but differed from the Stockton model in its cooling system and crawler assembly design. The military departments of several different European countries employed them during World War I. After the war, Holt continued to build the 75 as sales remained strong for a while. The 75 tractor was found to be as tough and reliable in farming as it was in long-distance heavy hauling or road construction. In 1921 the Holt 75 received its final design upgrades. Built only at Stockton, and still known as the T-8 series, the tractor acquired improvements to its radiator and undercarriage. But the tiller-wheel tractors' days were numbered, and only 67 of this redesigned unit left the Stockton plant before production came to an end in 1924. In all, approximately 4,620 Holt 75 tractors were produced, including the 442 built in Lincoln, England. Of the total, more than 2,000 were sold for military use.

Most of these machines have disappeared, but in 1999 three examples were found with a sunken vessel off the north coast of Scotland. The wreck occurred in 1917, while

HOLT BABY 30
Another Stockton-only-built tractor model was the Holt Baby 30, first introduced in 1912. Power was supplied by a four-cylinder 5-1/4x6-inch bore-and-stroke, valve-in-head gas motor. The Baby 30 lasted until 1916, with 301 examples being built, all in Stockton. *ECO Collection*

C.L. BEST 75 H.P. TRACKLAYER
The C.L. Best 75 H.P. Tracklayer was a brute of a tractor for its day. Tipping the scales at 28,000 pounds, it outweighed the Holt 120 by 1,500 pounds. Originally introduced in late 1912 as the C.L. Best 70 H.P. Tracklayer, it became the C.L.B. 75 in 1914. It was powered by a big Best-designed, four-cylinder 7-3/4x9-inch bore-and-stroke gas engine. The C.L.B. 70/75 tractors were originally built at Best's Elmhurst, California, facilities. By mid-1916, manufacturing was transferred to a new location in San Leandro. When production finally ended in 1919, approximately 734 C.L.B. 70/75 tractors had been built. Only a couple complete units are known to exist in the world today. *ECO Collection*

C.L. BEST "HUMPBACK" 30 H.P.
Between 1914 and 1915, C.L. Best built a special run of 45 tractors identified as the C.L.B. "Humpback" 30 H.P. Tracklayer. Unique to the Humpback 30 was its elevated drive sprocket design. It was primarily designed for orchard and vineyard cultivating work. This was the only time C.L. Best would attempt this type of track-drive arrangement in one of his designs. Today, only one of these special tractors is still in existence, and it is owned by the Fred C. Heidrick Ag History Center in Woodland, California. *Caterpillar, Inc. Corporate Archives*

the ship was en route from the east coast of England to continental Europe, and was probably caused by enemy attack. The valuable cargo consisted of three brand-new Holt 75 tractors manufactured in Lincoln, England, by Ruston & Hornsby Ltd., and a brand-new Clayton-Shuttleworth 100-horsepower tiller-wheel crawler tractor, also built in Lincoln. At the time of this writing, efforts are under way to salvage these tractors.

Holt produced an even larger tiller-wheel tractor that was the result of a government request for a heavy-duty artillery machine in the 20-ton range. The first prototype appeared in 1914 and was known as the Holt 120 Model A-PEP. Initially, a unique Holt six-cylinder, 7-1/2x8-inch bore-and-stroke gas engine of the "enclosed" type was installed, but after tests proved unsatisfactory, this engine was replaced by the six-cylinder Ell-head-design, Holt M-8

model, with the same bore and stroke as the former engine. By the time full production commenced in 1915, the tractor was referred to as the T-9 series, and was rated at 120-brake-horsepower and 70-drawbar-horsepower. The big Holt 120 weighed some 26,500 pounds, and shared many components with the Peoria Holt 75 being built at the same time. All 120s were built at the Peoria plant from 1915 to 1922, and of the 698 total shipped, records show that 676 were dispatched to the armed forces of the United States and Great Britain for military duties in World War I. Today, almost all of these tractors have been scrapped, and only two or three are known to still exist.

In addition to the large tiller-wheel tractors, Holt built two small models designed for use in orchards and vineyards. These were the Baby 30 and the 18 Midget, products of the Stockton factory. The Baby 30 was designed on similar lines to the larger 60 and 75 models, and utilized a four-cylinder Holt 5-1/4x6-inch bore-and-stroke, valve-in-head gas motor. Even smaller was the 18 Midget powered by a 4-1/2x5-1/2-inch bore-and-stroke Ell-head motor. Holt sold approximately 301 units of the Baby from 1912 to 1916, and 347 units of the Midget from 1914 to 1917.

BEST TILLER-WHEEL TRACTORS

The C.L. Best Gas Traction Company was founded in 1910 as the result of disagreements between the Holt Manufacturing Company and Clarence Leo (C.L.) Best while he was president of Holt's San Leandro plant. Two years earlier, C.L. Best's father, Daniel, had sold the family business, the Best Manufacturing Company, to Holt. As part of the agreement, C.L. Best was installed as the new president of the San Leandro plant. But C.L.'s management ideas were obstructed by Holt family members, many of whom reported to him at San Leandro, but also held seats on Holt's main Board of Directors—a totally unworkable situation. Frustrated, C.L. left the company, taking with him several key managers and engineers loyal to him, and established the C.L. Best Gas Traction Company at Elmhurst, California. The new company was financed by his father, Daniel, brother-in-law, Charles Q. Nelson, and several local farmers and friends.

Like his father's company before him, C.L. Best's new venture started business building large-wheel tractors. The most successful of these were the C.L.B. 60 H.P. and the C.L.B. 80 H.P., both powered by big six-cylinder Buffalo gas engines. After limited success with wheel tractors, and always keeping an eye on his chief competitor and former employer, C.L. Best and his team designed their first tiller-wheel crawler tractor and launched it in 1912. Identified as the C.L.B. 70 H.P. Tracklayer, the machine featured many advanced design improvements not found on the Holt machines. For example, steering was accomplished through a differential drive that maintained power to both tracks at all times, one being driven slower than the other during turning. (The Holt tractors drove their tracks independently, disconnecting the drive to one side or the other to effect turning.) Best also used high-grade steel in critical areas throughout the machine. The prototype tractor's gas engine was a big six-cylinder Buffalo unit, the same type

used by the company in its round wheel tractors. At that same time, however, Best's engineers were perfecting a new gasoline engine designed in-house. This engine became available in July 1913, and was installed in the Tracklayers thereafter. The four-cylinder, 70-horsepower gas engine boasted a 7-3/4x9-inch bore and stroke. After further modifications, design improvements, and more power developed from its engine, the 70 Tracklayer was upgraded to the 75 Tracklayer in 1914.

Also in 1914, C.L. Best introduced the 30 H.P. "Humpback," a small tiller-wheel tractor designed for orchard and nursery work. Its distinguishing feature, an elevated drive sprocket raised above the rear idler roller, gave the tractor the appearance of its namesake. This tractor was an early example of what is known today as a "high-drive," a design adopted by Caterpillar for its large tractors over six decades later. It was the only tractor of this design made by Best, and only 45 were produced up to 1915.

In a very short space of time, the Best 75 gained an excellent reputation as a tough and reliable tractor. It emerged as a formidable competitor for the Holt 75, and its sales allowed the Best company to prosper. By 1916, C.L. Best was able to purchase his father's former plant in San Leandro, vacated by Holt three years earlier, and expand his business into the larger factory. Production of the Best 75 continued up to 1919, by which time 734 had been built. A few of these were sold as the C.L.B. 75 H.P. Round Wheel tractor with 90-inch driving wheels instead of crawler tracks.

A larger Best tiller-wheel tractor, the C.L.B. 90 H.P. Tracklayer, was presented by Best in 1916. This massive piece of iron carried a Best four-cylinder, 8x9-inch bore-and-stroke gas engine and a heavier main frame. The 90's crawler tracks were 2 feet longer than the 75 model, and each crawler frame was carried on seven rollers compared with five on the 75 model. Only 39 of the Best 90 tractors are recorded as being sold when it was withdrawn from production in 1917. An even larger and less successful tractor was the C.L. Best 120 H.P. Tracklayer. One of these was built in 1916, and four more in 1917, but no records have been found to indicate where these tractors were shipped, or for what purpose they were used.

CHAPTER TWO

CATERPILLER TRACTOR CO. BACKGROUND

By the early 1920s, the crawler tractor had established itself as an essential part of farming operations. Gone were the cumbersome, inefficient clanking monsters of the early days, and the tiller-wheel tractors, still being produced up to the mid-1920s, were losing their market. Tiller-wheel tractors had worked well, and done the job they were designed to do, but in the changing world of the early 1920s, their wide turning radius and awkward maneuverability made them obsolete. The fact that their market lasted as long as it did was only because of faithful repeat-order customers who resisted changing to the nimble two-crawler tractors now on the scene.

As farming became more sophisticated, manufacturers worked to fill the needs of the modern farmer looking for efficient equipment. World War I was behind them, and manufacturers could no longer rely on bulk orders from the armed forces. So they designed and launched new tractor models to entice farmers and other civilian users to modernize their fleets. In many farming areas, much persuasion was still necessary to convert owners from horses and mules to mechanized power.

During World War I, Holt had been perfecting tractors that dispensed with the tiller wheel and steered entirely with clutches and brakes. The tillerless concept actually

BEST 60
Introduced in 1919, the C.L. Best 60 Tracklayer was a key turning point in crawler tractor design. The Best 60 essentially replaced the "40" Tracklayer in the company's tractor lineup. Power was supplied by a Best-designed four-cylinder 6-1/2x8-1/2 bore-and-stroke gasoline engine, rated at 60-belt horsepower. This fully restored "60" is of early 1919 vintage. Owner: Joseph A. Heidrick, Sr. Foundation. *ECO*

HOLT 45 "MULEY"
The Holt 45 "muley" (Model T-10) Caterpillar tractor was built both at the Peoria and Stockton manufacturing locations. Pictured is a Peoria-built machine produced from 1914 to 1919. It was powered by a four-cylinder Holt M-9, 6x7-inch bore-and-stroke, valve-in-head gasoline motor. The Peoria tractors utilized a different radiator design than that found on the Stockton machines. Approximately 652 Holt 45 muleys of all types were built in Peoria. Of this total, 165 units were classified as commercial domestic production, with the rest allocated for military uses. *ECO Collection*

originated from one of Holt's mechanics who, while assembling tiller-wheel tractors, discovered he could move them around without the aid of the tiller wheel. He drove one out of the factory in a successful demonstration to show how well a crawler tractor could function without the extra front wheel. Soon after this event, Holt brought out its first prototype non-tiller crawler in 1913. Known as the Holt 20-30 (series T-5), it was powered by an M-4 four-cylinder, 6x7-inch bore-and-stroke, Doman Tee-Head gas engine rated at 30-brake horsepower. Eleven of these tractors were produced before some design improvements caused its evolution into the Holt 45 (T-10) in 1914. This 45 model was different from the earlier Holt 45, which steered by tiller wheel. Farmers nicknamed these early tillerless tractors "muleys," a farming term for a cow without horns.

In 1915 the U.S. Army put the new Holt 45 through a rigorous testing program and the tractor came through with flying colors. Consequently, the Army sent large numbers of these tractors to the battlefields of Europe during World War I, where the French and the U.S. utilized them to keep supply lines open and artillery equipment on the move. The tractors operated successfully in some of the worst conditions imaginable—hauling heavy loads off-road in water and mud, traveling through thick brush or over fallen trees, and often going without adequate maintenance. Forty-two of the Holt 45s shipped to the Army in 1917 and 1918 were special versions known as the Model 45 E-HVS (T-12) Armored Artillery Tractor. These were completely covered in armor plating, and their frame was of cast-steel design. However, the engine was the same as the standard model. In all the company sold 1,891 Holt 45 tractors, including the special military versions, by the time production ended in 1920.

Holt introduced another armor-plated tractor in 1917. It was the 10-Ton Model 55 Artillery Tractor (series

HOLT 45 "MULEY"

The Stockton-built Holt 45 "muley" (Model T-10) tractors were produced from 1915 through 1920. They utilized the same M-9 motors found in the Peoria machines, but utilized a different radiator design. The Stockton "45" could also be ordered in a low-profile orchard configuration. Production of Stockton-built T-10 tractors amounted to 1,239. Total production from both plants was approximately 1,891. Pictured in 2000 is a vintage 1917 Holt 45, No. 20527. Owner: Peter M. Holt. *ECO*

HOLT 10-TON "55"

Holt first introduced its 10-Ton series of Caterpillar crawlers in 1917 as the Model 55 Artillery Tractor. It was in production until 1919. Covered in full armor plating, it was powered by a Holt M-11, four-cylinder 6-1/2x7-inch bore-and-stroke, valve-in-head gasoline engine. Pictured in early 1918 is an armored "55," known within Holt Manufacturing as the T-16. *Courtesy Caterpillar, Inc. Corporate Archives*

T-16), powered by a four-cylinder Holt M-11 gasoline engine, with a 6-1/2x7-inch bore and stroke, rated at 55-brake horsepower and 40-drawbar horsepower. It was faster and more powerful than the earlier Holt 45, which it eventually replaced for military use. The military continued to purchase the 10-Ton military version in large numbers up to 1919. To cope with the demand, Holt had to subcontract this tractor to the Chandler Motor Car Company of Cleveland, Ohio, which assembled 700 units

under license. Records show that some 2,803 Holt 10-Ton Artillery tractors were eventually sold.

The muley tractor concept, thoroughly tested on the battlefields of Europe, was proven and accepted. As steering clutches and brakes were improved, the tiller wheel as an aid to steering was found unnecessary, even on the largest tractors. The successful wartime application of Holt's 45 and 10-Ton 55 military tractors prompted the company to introduce a similar-sized tractor for civilian use immediately after the war. A prototype 10-Ton (T-16), with the same engine found in the military version, was tested in 1918, and full production commenced in 1919 at the Peoria plant. The commercial 10-Ton retained the unusual two-part crawler bogey frame favored by the Army. The split frame, with each part carrying a number of track rollers, was believed to result in a better ride at higher speeds and possess better trench-crossing capabilities. The 40-drawbar horsepower tractor was listed with a shipping weight of 20,500 pounds,

but the operating weight varied slightly depending on how the tractor was rigged. Track gauge was 60 inches.

The Holt 10-Ton was equipped with a three-speed transmission, but the speeds could be varied depending on how the tractor was initially ordered. Standard speeds were 1.67 miles per hour in first, 2.2 miles per hour in second, and 3 miles per hour, in third. However, for hauling lighter loads at faster speeds, the optional gear ratios gave speeds of 1.67 miles per hour, 3 miles per hour and 4.78 miles per hour. These latter speeds were particularly attractive to customers in the hauling business, who purchased a good proportion of tractors in the 1920s. A Caterpillar tractor hauling eight or more dump wagons or transport trailers was a common sight. Haulage by crawler tractor was, of course, wiped out with the advent of off-highway rubber-tired haulage a decade later. After that time, crawler tractors were offered with only their standard gear ratios providing powerful low speeds for heavy-duty dozing, ripping, or scraper duties.

In 1924 the 10-Ton received some minor modifications, including a newly designed radiator with the Holt name cast on both sides instead of only on the front as in the former models. The updated 10-Ton tractor was a big seller for the company, and this model would continue as the Caterpillar 10-Ton tractor following the formation of Caterpillar Tractor Company in 1925.

Holt launched a special "Western" version of the 10-Ton in 1921 (series TS-21). Designed for western farms, it differed from the standard model in that its undercarriage was shorter, and its crawler shoes were wider to reduce

HOLT 10-TON (LEFT)
A domestic version of the Holt 10-Ton (Model T-16) was introduced in mid-1918, with full production commencing in 1919. The 10-Ton would eventually take the place of the Holt 45, though both tractors were built at the same time for a short period. All Model T-16 tractors, including military variations, were powered by the Holt M-11 gasoline motor. Owner: Joseph A. Heidrick, Sr. Foundation. *ECO*

HOLT WESTERN 10-TON (BELOW)
Between 1921 and 1923, Holt Manufacturing produced the Western 10-Ton (Model TS-21). Built to counter the C.L. Best 60's popularity in the western United States, it was powered by a Holt M-21, four-cylinder 6-1/2x7-inch bore-and-stroke, valve-in-head motor. The engine, as well as the tractor itself, was only manufactured at the Stockton facilities. Its undercarriage was developed from the Holt 45 "muley," and shared many of the same castings. Only 152 examples of this unique Caterpillar tractor were ever produced. *ECO Collection*

HOLT 10-TON

In late 1924, the Holt 10-Ton Caterpillar tractor received a revised radiator casting design. It featured the word "HOLT" cast vertically down the radiator's sides. After the tractor became a Caterpillar Tractor Company model in April 1925, it would receive a revised casting with "10 TON" on the sides. *ECO Collection*

compaction. It also featured an upgraded Holt M-21, four-cylinder engine with a 6-1/2x7-inch bore and stroke, and its sheet metal was of a clean and more compact design. The Holt "Western" 10-Ton tractors were in production until 1923. Records show that 152 were sold, a disappointingly low number for a tractor designed to take on the vast western farms in competition with the well-established Best tractors. The "Western" 10-Ton was built at the Stockton plant, but all the other commercial 10-Ton tractors were built at Peoria.

A smaller tractor, the Holt 5-ton (series T-11), had a military background similar to its larger brother. Introduced in 1917 as the 5-Ton Artillery Tractor, it was powered with a Holt M-12 gas engine, with a 4-3/4x6-inch bore and stroke, rated at 40-brake horsepower and 25-drawbar horsepower. With the exception of three produced in the Holt factory, the military 5-Ton tractors were built under license agreements by Maxwell Motor Car Company of Detroit, Michigan, and by Reo Motor Car Company of Lansing, Michigan. These two companies produced 2,193 and 1,477

HOLT 5-TON
The original Holt 5-Ton (Model T-11), like the 10-Ton, was designed primarily for military duties at first. Released in 1917 as the 5-Ton Artillery Tractor Model 1917, it was powered by a Holt M-12, four-cylinder 4-3/4x6-inch bore-and-stroke, valve-in-head gasoline engine. Domestic versions of the Model T-11 would start rolling off the assembly line in 1919. All commercial T-11 Holt 5-Ton tractors were built in Peoria from 1919 on. *ECO Collection*

HOLT 5-TON
Starting in 1921, Holt built the first prototype Model T-29 tractors. By mid-1923, the final design was reached that would become the successor to the old Model T-11. Built only in Stockton, this light green Holt 5-Ton (Model T-29) featured a riveted undercarriage track frame, and a fuel tank mounted in front of the operator. The engine was a Stockton-built Holt M-29, four-cylinder 4-3/4x6-inch bore-and-stroke, valve-in-head motor. Production ended on the Stockton machine in 1924 with approximately 213 units manufactured. Pictured in 1999 is a vintage 1924 model carrying serial No. S-50099. Owner: Joseph A. Heidrick, Sr. Foundation. *ECO*

CATERPILLAR 5-TON
In late 1924 the Stockton riveted-frame 5-Ton tractor was replaced by the Peoria-built Holt New 5-Ton "Caterpillar" Tractor (Model T-29). This model featured a cast-steel undercarriage, as well as a new radiator design. The engine was the same M-29 unit found in the Stockton machine. In April 1925, this model became the Caterpillar 5-Ton. Separate chassis and engine serial numbers were issued early in this model's production life. But the practice ended with M-29 motor No. 53846 on October 13, 1925. Pictured is a vintage 1926 tractor carrying chassis serial No. 44487. Total production (which ended in 1926) of this Peoria-built model series amounted to 1,500 tractors. *ECO*

HOLT 2-TON
Introduced in 1921, the Holt 2-Ton (Model T-35) was the smallest "muley" tractor designed by the company. It was originally built at the Stockton plant with riveted track frames, and a Holt M-35, four-cylinder 4x5-1/2-inch bore-and-stroke, valve-in-head gasoline motor. Most of these riveted-framed, 2-Ton tractors were painted light green, though a few were shipped dressed in gray. This Stockton-built 2-Ton ended production in mid-1924 with 1,350 units shipped. Pictured is a vintage 1923 model carrying serial No. S26267. *ECO*

of the Holt 5-Ton tractors, respectively, through 1918. Most of these tractors carried the letters U.S.A. instead of the usual Holt name on their radiators.

The following year, Holt's 5-Ton (T-11) went into full production for civilian use. In addition, some T-11s previously built during the war for the military returned to Holt for conversion to commercial models, complete with new serial numbers. About 300 of these tractors were resold up to 1921. Not counting the revamped units, Holt built approximately 2,425 5-Ton (T-11) tractors up to 1923, when this model was discontinued in favor of the new 5-Ton (T-29).

Before commercial sales commenced, six prototype and two special export 5-Ton T-29 versions had been tested over the previous two years. Built in the Stockton factory, this tractor's 25-drawbar horsepower engine was basically the same as the previous model, but the tractor had a very different appearance. The fuel tank was now mounted ahead of the operator and incorporated into the front engine hood. The undercarriage and track frames were riveted construction, and the track gauge was 48-3/4 inches. The three-speed transmission gave speeds of 1.51 miles per hour in first, 3 miles per hour in second, and 5.71 miles per hour in top gear, the last a very high speed for a crawler tractor in those days. Overall, the bare tractor weighed 9,400 pounds. This particular 5-Ton model had a relatively short life, with only 213 units sold before it was superseded by a revised version in late 1924. The new version was known as the New 5-Ton Caterpillar Tractor, Model T-29, and was a product of the Peoria, Illinois, plant. It was distinguished by the Holt name cast into the radiator sides, rather than marked with stencil cutout letters as on previous Stockton-built machines. The New 5-Ton was so well accepted that it was carried forward as the Caterpillar 5-Ton after the establishment of Caterpillar Tractor Company in 1925.

The third tractor in Holt's early 1920s product line was the 2-Ton Model T-35, launched in 1921. Smaller than the other two, it featured a unique overhead-camshaft Holt M-35 four-cylinder gasoline engine, with 4x5-1/2-inch bore and stroke. This engine produced 15-drawbar horsepower and 25-belt horsepower when running at its rated speed of 1,000 rpm. This initial 2-Ton model was distinguished by its riveted undercarriage together with the Holt name on the radiator in stencil cutout form. Records show that about 1,350 units of this model were sold. In 1924, Holt introduced a new 2-Ton tractor boasting a much stronger under-carriage of cast-steel construction, and the radiator housing now displayed the Holt name cast on the sides. The 2-Ton was available with narrow (38-inch) or wide (52-inch) track gauges. The redesign added some 1,300 pounds to the orig-inal 2-ton weight of the tractor. It was equipped with a three-speed transmission, offering speeds of 2.12 miles per hour, 3 miles per hour, and 5.25 miles per hour. This tractor would join the Holt 5-Ton and 10-Ton models as Holt's three-model contribution to the new tractor lineup marketed by the Caterpillar Tractor Company after its formation in 1925.

Meanwhile, the Best company was making parallel developments with non-tiller-wheel tractors. One of the first tillerless tractors Best offered was the 40-brake-horse-power C.L. Best 40 Tracklayer, introduced in 1914. Designed to compete with the Holt 45, it was a little lighter and had 5 fewer horsepower. This model proved popular, with the company selling approximately 747 units for civil-ian use by 1919 when production ceased. In 1918 the com-pany made a special version of this tractor, the C.L. Best 45. This model packed 5 additional horsepower to equal the Holt machine, but records show that only one of this model appears to have been built.

A couple of other Best tillerless tractors experienced limited success during this period. In 1916 the C.L. Best 16 Pony Tracklayer was introduced as an orchard tractor, or small farm tractor. The company hoped its lower price would attract those farmers not yet converted to mecha-nized power. Also known as the Pony 8-16, it was powered by a four-cylinder Best, 4-3/8x5-1/4-inch bore-and-stroke gas engine rated at 8-drawbar horsepower and 16-belt horsepower. This little tractor was well designed, but its timing worked against it. The company launched it in the

HOLT 2-TON
Starting in June 1924, a newly designed Holt 2-Ton (Model T-35) began shipping from the Peoria plant, replacing the Stockton machine. This new design featured cast-steel track frames, as well as "HOLT" cast into the radiator sides. After this version of the 2-Ton became a Caterpillar Tractor Company model in April 1925, the radiator "HOLT" castings were still utilized for a couple of months until the existing parts inventories were exhausted. During the early life of this tractor model, separate serial numbers were issued to the chassis and engine. This practice stopped on October 13, 1925, when engine numbering ended with M-35 motor serial No. 81401. Pictured in 2000 is a Peoria-built, 1925 vintage 2-Ton, serial No. 71146 (motor 81258). Owner: Charles Bogar. *ECO*

middle of World War I, when there was an acute shortage of steel available for civilian use. Customers placed over 50 orders but the company could not fill them because of war demands. Records show only two built in 1916 and anoth-er in 1917. Best tried again with another small tractor in 1917, the C.L. Best 30 Tracklayer, but this model was only marginally more successful than the earlier 16 Pony trac-tor. It was powered by a four-cylinder Best, 5-1/4x6-1/4-inch bore-and-stroke gas engine of 16-drawbar horsepower and 30-belt horsepower. The C.L. Best 30 did not extend beyond its introduction year, and only 15 units sold.

The C.L. Best model just described was actually one of three different Best "30" models launched by the company at different times. The first was the short-lived Humpback 30 introduced in 1914 (see Chapter 1). Then in 1921, Best brought out an entirely different tractor, but still labeled it the Best 30 Tracklayer. This much-improved model even-tually became the Caterpillar Thirty, described later. After the unsuccessful 30 Tracklayer in 1917, Best introduced its replacement the following year, the more popular Best 25 Tracklayer. A smaller version of the successful 40 Tracklayer, this 25-horsepower model was almost identical in appearance to its larger brother. Some 300 of the 25 Tracklayer were sold over a two-year period.

Best's tractor sales during World War I were decidedly lacking when compared with the large quantities being shipped by Holt for military purposes. But prosperity for

CATERPILLAR 2-TON
A short time after the Holt 2-Ton became the Caterpillar 2-Ton, its radiator casting was changed to read "2 TON," after the extra "HOLT" cast parts were used up. Other than that, the tractors were virtually identical. Pictured in 1999 is a fully restored 1928 Caterpillar 2-Ton, serial No. 75575. In all, there were approximately 8,989 Peoria-built 2-Ton tractors manufactured when production ended in 1928. Owner: Ron Miller. *ECO*

Best lay just around the corner. Probably the biggest milestone in the Best company's history occurred in 1919 when the company launched the C.L. Best 60 Tracklayer. This model turned out to be one of the most famous crawler tractors ever built. It would keep the C.L. Best Tractor Company in business during the difficult years following the war, and after the Caterpillar Tractor Company was formed in 1925, it would become the legendary Caterpillar Sixty.

The launch of the C.L. Best 60 Tracklayer marked a significant turning point in the evolution of the crawler tractor. Some of the features that made it such a standout performer were its oscillating crawler frames, some 36 bearings located at critical points throughout the machine, multiple-disc enclosed steering clutches, and a strong frame capable of withstanding lots of abuse. It was powered by a four-cylinder overhead-valve Best 6-1/2x8-1/2-inch bore-and-stroke gas engine of 35- drawbar horsepower and 60-belt horsepower. This engine ran at a slow 650 rpm, one of the slowest engines fitted to an early crawler tractor. The standard transmission on the first Best 60s provided only two forward speeds, but a three-speed transmission was available as an option. By 1923 power

output had increased to 40-drawbar horsepower, and the three-speed transmission was standard. Typical of most tractors, the Best 60 gained in weight over the years it was produced. Starting out at approximately 17,500 pounds, its weight increased in several increments to 20,500 when it became a Caterpillar machine.

Another evolution took place with the driver seat arrangement. Initially the tractor featured a low, orchard-type seat that overhung the rear end. Although this was satisfactory for most applications, it was dangerous for logging operators, who would be thrown around traversing rough terrain in the springy, overhung seat. Best modified the design by raising the seating position above fender level and making it a two-seater affixed to a solid frame running across the width of the tractor. The new arrangement was first aimed at loggers, and was called the Model 60 Cruiser, but starting in 1922, the high-seat version became standard for the 60.

In the field, the Best 60 was regarded as the toughest and most-reliable tractor available. The company extended its marketing efforts beyond agricultural markets into many other industries, some of which had never before

BEST 60

From any angle, the Best 60 was a well-proportioned crawler tractor for its day. Most of the early tractors were supplied with the tailseat configuration for agricultural fieldwork. In 1920 a high mounted operator's seat option became available. Owner: Joseph A. Heidrick, Sr. Foundation. *ECO*

been mechanized. Its heavy-duty crawler power found favor in logging, mining, and construction applications, and proved to be a prime mover for hauling earth wagons along rough haul roads. The Sixty also made long-distance hauling possible. Trains of wagons were able to carry supplies and materials to distant construction sites, oil fields, and other remote locations previously accessed only by horses and mules.

In 1921, Best added a smaller tractor to its product line, the Best 30 Tracklayer. It was designed along lines similar to the popular 60 model, and replaced the earlier Best 25. At approximately half the size of its big brother, the Best 30 carried a four-cylinder Best, 4-3/4x6-1/2-inch bore-and-stroke motor, rated at 20-drawbar horsepower and 30-belt horsepower when running at a rated 800 rpm. Like its larger brother, the 30 was initially equipped with a two-speed transmission, but later versions offered three speeds. And like its big brother, its operator's seat evolved from the low, overhung "tailseat" type designed for orchard use, to the more rigid bench-type seat raised above the fenders. The Best 30 gained an enviable reputation for reliability, and was equally suited for work on the farm, in the woods, or on

construction sites. Sales proved very encouraging, and it turned out to be another winner for the company.

The popular 30 tractor was offered with a number of operating attachments, such as a front power takeoff (PTO), with which it could perform the duties of a stationary engine. In this configuration, the hand crank handle was extended to the rear instead of the usual front position. The Best 30 could also be purchased with either a 43-3/4-inch standard track gauge or with a wide 60-3/4-inch track gauge. That was even a tad wider than the big Hot 10-Ton! This super-wide gauge tractor could be fitted with wide shoes, making it nearly invincible on steep hillsides. And the same tractor could work on marshy ground in areas where other tractors feared to tread. Like the Best 60, the 30 was carried forward into the new Caterpillar Tractor Company line after 1925, becoming the Caterpillar Thirty.

CATERPILLAR TRACTOR COMPANY ESTABLISHED

The merger of the two leading tractor builders of the 1920s to establish the Caterpillar Tractor Company in 1925 marked the culmination of a series of events that unfolded over several years. The seeds of the merger were

BEST 60 "LOGGING CRUISER"
The Best 60 "Logging Cruiser" was first offered to the forestry industry in 1920. The "Cruiser" featured all of the main attributes of the standard "60," plus the following: a three-speed transmission geared for four-miles-per-hour top speed, a selective gear shift at the driver side, a hand brake in addition to the foot brakes, top-mounted operator's seat for two, a collapsible top, special pullbar at the rear, a tow hook in the front, a radiator guard (not shown), a larger fuel tank, and a cushioned equalizer bar. *ECO Collection*

planted immediately after the end of World War I, when marketing conditions drastically changed for the two famous tractor companies. Wartime production for Holt had been very rewarding. Almost everything Holt produced in the war years went to the military. Thousands of tractors were ordered by the U.S., British, and French armies, and the company could hardly meet demands. Holt's own production lines were filled, and in order to cope with demand, the company commissioned other manufacturers to build tractors under license.

Best also achieved extensive sales during the war, but not at Holt's level. Although Best had assurances from the government that it could continue to supply crawler tractors for agriculture during the war years, production numbers were not great due to the depressed state of the economy on the home front. Models launched during the war were hindered by the same circumstances. Although the company was poised to launch its most successful tractors (Best 30 and 60) when the war ended, it was not in a strong position by that time.

When the armistice was signed in November 1918, World War I was over: Great news for the soldiers on the battle fronts, but not so good for industries at home that had depended on government orders for survival. The tractor industry was one of the hardest hit. Holt had made factory expansions during the war years to achieve high-volume military production. This came to an abrupt end when the U.S. Ordnance Department canceled all outstanding orders. The cancellations were very significant because the company had delivered only 9,771 tractors out of a total of 24,791 ordered by the military.

Canceled orders were not Holt's only problem. With the war over, the military could no longer use all the tractors they owned, and started disposing of them wherever they could. Many went to the Bureau of Public Roads, which shipped them all over the United States. Others were sold at pennies on the dollar as Army Surplus. Consequently, the market was flooded with little-used ex-army tractors in excellent condition, some of them brand new. Farmers and other customers had no incentive to

BEST 60 "SNOW SPECIAL"
Around 1923, the Best 60 was offered in a factory "Snow Special" configuration for extreme cold weather usage. It featured an enclosed cab with a heating coil operated from the exhaust, dual front-mounted headlights, an engine hood with canvas curtains on the side, a front tow hook, and a frost pan mounted beneath the motor. This last feature, when used with the radiator's adjustable curtain, controlled the temperature of the motor. *ECO Collection*

place orders from the manufacturers when they could obtain these tractors for next to nothing.

As if these problems were not enough, Holt found itself with a line of military products unsuitable for the agriculture and construction markets. And being so involved with massive government orders, it had neglected to keep in touch with the needs of domestic customers. Its heavy and powerful tractors designed for military purposes were ill-suited for work in the fields. The end of World War I had thus left Holt in a precarious position.

Meanwhile, Best had worked with farmers throughout the war years and produced machines that were well suited to farming needs. It had also expanded its dealer network, and was confident that its new, well-designed 30 and 60 tractors would gain markets. In anticipation of expansion, Best changed its corporate name to the C.L. Best Tractor Company in 1920 to better reflect its product. Yet, as mentioned, the war had left the company in a weak

financial position and without adequate resources to market and properly support its machines. Like its competitor Holt, it also suffered from a market flooded with the ex-military tractors. So in the early 1920s, even after so much initial success, both Holt and Best were facing huge debts and the possibility of failure. Operating capital had been obtained on long lines of credit from financial institutions, and often these loans were refinanced by borrowing from other institutions, compounding the situation. Benjamin Holt's sudden death in December 1920 left company management scrambling to maintain production, keep track of financial matters, and reorganize the company.

The two companies' weak financial situations and bleak prospects were scrutinized by their respective key financial institutions. The Boston firm of Bond and Goodwin was Holt's main financier, while Best's chief lending institution was Pierce, Fair and Company of San Francisco. These firms, represented on the tractor companies' boards of directors, realized that long-term prospects looked good, and both companies had the capability to design and market products that could be applied in a wide range of markets. But somehow both companies had to overcome a short-term financial crunch, a weak economy, and the glut of military tractors flooding the market.

The financial lending institutions began to assume more control of the situation. Thomas Baxter, a banker from Bond and Goodwin, was elected president of the Holt Manufacturing Company, filling the position left vacant by Benjamin Holt's death. Baxter undertook drastic measures to prevent the ailing Holt company from going under. He streamlined production, cut the large 120 model from the product line, and hastened the introduction of smaller tractors, better aligned to agricultural needs. He also initiated an extensive advertising program directed to road builders who, at that time, could take advantage of a $1 billion federal highway building fund. But all these actions cost money, and despite Baxter's strong efforts, the company sank further into debt.

Harry Fair, who represented Pierce, Fair and Company on the C.L. Best Gas Traction Company board, started to take some action on behalf of that firm. Earlier, Fair had assisted C.L. Best in financing the expansion of the company. A major reorganization of the company's finances in 1920 resulted in a name change from the C.L. Best Gas Traction Company to the C.L. Best Tractor Company. Not only had Fair invested substantial sums of company money in the Best company, but he had personal funds involved as well. In exploring the options for survival, he initiated conversations with Pliny Holt and Murray Baker, head of Holt's Peoria plant, and suggested that the two companies might merge. After all, he said, "there appears to be ample market for one big tractor maker, but not

two." As an incentive, and to further demonstrate his confidence in the idea of one large company, he offered the full financial backing of Pierce, Fair and Company.

Merging the two companies made a lot of sense, allowing them to combine their engineering strengths and customer bases, rationalize procedures, trim excess employees, and eliminate duplication of dealerships. The result would be a stronger, more efficient company with adequate resources to sell and service its products.

The Articles of Incorporation of Caterpillar Tractor Company were filed with the Secretary of State of California on April 15, 1925, by the law firm of Chickering & Gregory, San Francisco. The five-page document, No. 113767, contained details of the proposed new company, including its purpose:

> To manufacture, produce, buy, sell, import, export, or otherwise acquire, dispose of, or deal in tractors, harvesters, machinery, agricultural implements, and vehicles of every kind and character.

Over the subsequent few months, the shareholders of the two companies approved the proposition, and the Superior Court of the State of California ordered the voluntary dissolution of both companies. Thus, the names Holt Manufacturing Company and C.L. Best Tractor Company became history, and in their places the new venture, Caterpillar Tractor Company, was born. This is the same company that today, under the name Caterpillar, Inc., manufactures a vast range of construction, mining, logging, and farm equipment from the smallest mini excavator to the largest trucks ever to roam the earth. The name "Caterpillar," therefore, no longer describes a type of machine—it refers to products produced by Caterpillar, Inc. and its subsidiaries. Who would have predicted that the intense rivalry of the two proud companies, Holt and Best, would end in amalgamation, and that the chosen name for the new company would become the most well-known name in the heavy equipment industry?

BEST 30 TRACKLAYER
Following in the footsteps of the "60" was the C.L. Best 30 Tracklayer, in 1921. This smaller version of the "60" was powered by a Best four-cylinder 4-3/4x6-1/2-inch bore-and-stroke, valve-in-head gasoline engine. The model would become the Caterpillar Thirty in 1925. This tractor is a 1922 vintage Best 30 (S.N. S1514). Owner: Doug Veerkamp. *ECO*

I mmediately following the merger of the Holt Manufacturing Company and C.L. Best Tractor Company in 1925, the management of the new Caterpillar Tractor Company followed through with proposed plans to streamline its operations and marketing network. They eliminated duplicate procedures resulting from the merger, reduced the number of employees, and consolidated the dealer network. Where former Holt and Best dealers served the same locations, now there would be a single dealer, more efficiently representing the full line of Caterpillar products.

To launch the new company's first product line, Caterpillar chose existing models from the former companies' lines, two from Best and three from Holt. The colors selected for the new lineup were gray with red trim. The old Best colors of black, gold, and red were now history. The five tractors in the new Caterpillar lineup were the following:

1. The former Holt 2-Ton, originally introduced in 1921 and recently upgraded in 1924, became the Caterpillar 2-Ton.
2. The former Holt 5-Ton, which had its origins as a military tractor in 1917, became the Caterpillar 5-Ton. This model was sold as a civilian tractor from 1919 onward, and had just been upgraded in 1924 to the New 5-Ton.
3. The former Holt 10-Ton, also with origins as a military tractor, and sold as a civilian unit from 1919, became the

THIRTY
The Best 30 Tracklayer officially became a Caterpillar Thirty on April 15, 1925. The Caterpillar version featured a gray paint scheme trimmed in red, with the word "THIRTY" cast into the radiator sides. Model production continued in San Leandro (S.N. prefix S), and commenced in Peoria (S.N. prefix PS) in 1926. Pictured in 1999 is a fully restored San Leandro–built 1928 Thirty, serial No. S6387. Owner: Doug Veerkamp. *ECO*

THIRTY
Caterpillar Thirty tractors could be ordered with the regular high-mounted operator's seat, or a rear overhanging "orchard" tailseat configuration. When the Thirty was equipped with a tailseat, the fuel tank was mounted directly in front of the operator for better visibility to the left and right of the tractor. This tailseat Thirty from 1999 is a late vintage 1931 model, serial No. PS13604, manufactured in Peoria. After December 7, 1931, the standard Caterpillar tractor color became Hi-Way Yellow, trimmed in black. The optional paint was gray, trimmed in black. *ECO*

Caterpillar 10-Ton. This tractor had also been updated in 1924.

4. The former Best 30, originally introduced in 1921, became the Caterpillar Thirty.
5. The former Best 60, originally introduced in 1919, became the Caterpillar Sixty.

The new five-model lineup did not last long. First to be dropped was the 10-Ton. Although it was a well-liked and successful tractor in the field, and even though it had received some updates the previous year, management withdrew it from the line to reduce manufacturing costs. They believed it was competing in the same markets as the model Sixty and was more expensive to build because of its complicated two-part crawler bogey undercarriage and array of individual parts. The Caterpillar 10-Ton was dropped after only eight months of production in 1925, during which time 454 units left the Peoria plant. Total production of the 10-Ton tractor in both its Holt and Caterpillar guises was 6,437, including 2,803 built as Artillery Tractors.

Next to go was the 5-ton. Although it had sold well, it was considered by the forward-thinking Caterpillar management to be outmoded when compared with the company's Thirty tractor. Why take up valuable manufacturing space for two similar-sized tractors when one was inferior to the other? So production of the 5-Ton ceased toward the end of 1926, by which time 1,147 Caterpillar units, following some 353 Holt versions, had been assembled in the Peoria plant.

The small Caterpillar 2-Ton tractor had a much longer life in the new Caterpillar line than its 5-Ton and 10-Ton siblings. Starting out as the new Holt 2-Ton in 1924, production continued until the end of 1928. Apart from a new radiator casting replacing the Holt name with "2-TON" on its sides, the tractor design remained unchanged over this period. The 2-Ton proved very popular in all farming applications, and its compact dimensions were especially suited to orchard and vineyard use. As a result, 8,989 units were built, and its success helped provide the company with financial resources to develop the more advanced machines soon to follow.

THIRTY
This immaculate Stockton-built 1928 Caterpillar Thirty "Swamp Special" (S.N. S7021) is equipped with the optional 30-inch angle steel track shoes for higher flotation in wet working areas. Track spacing on this configuration was 60-3/4 inches between centers, instead of the standard 43-3/4-inch spacing. Although a Thirty of this vintage should be painted gray, trimmed in red, tractors built after December 7, 1931, were dressed just like this. Many of today's owners choose the Hi-Way Yellow paint over the gray for aesthetic reasons. Owner: Doug Veerkamp. *ECO*

The two former Best models in the initial Caterpillar lineup fared much better than the Holt models. The smaller of the two, the Caterpillar Thirty, continued to gain in popularity throughout the 1920s. Starting life in 1921 at Best's factory in San Leandro, California, it continued in production at that location after 1925 as the Caterpillar Thirty until 1930. Meanwhile, in 1926, a second production line for the Thirty was set up at the Peoria, Illinois, plant, where space was now available from the former production line of the discontinued 5-Ton model. Peoria built the Thirty up to 1932, when its production ceased. Different serial number prefixes were used to identify the Thirty's location of manufacture. San Leandro–built tractors were designated the S-series, beginning with serial No. S1001. Tractors built at Peoria had a 'PS' serial number prefix. A total number of 23,739 Best 30/Caterpillar Thirty tractors were built at both plants, making it by far the most popular crawler tractor for Caterpillar up to that time.

The Caterpillar Sixty enjoyed similar success. This model changed colors from the former Best black and gold to the new gray and red livery. When Best merged to form Caterpillar on April 15, 1925, the Best factory possessed a small inventory of components cast with Best part numbers and radiators with the name BEST cast in them. Consequently, tractors carrying the Best name on their radiators were sold as Caterpillar machines until all the old inventory was used up. Just when this occurred is not documented.

Sales flourished, and production of the Sixty continued in the San Leandro plant through 1930. In addition, a new production line was established in 1925 at Peoria where manufacture continued until 1931, with one final tractor produced in 1932. The Sixty tractors built in San Leandro started in 1919 with the serial No. 101A. Those built in Peoria starting in 1925 were christened with a PA serial number prefix. Combined sales figures for the Sixty tractors built at both plants numbered some 18,931 units.

Caterpillar actively followed its established policy of maintaining its position at the cutting edge of tractor development by frequently introducing new updated models. From the late 1920s to the early 1930s, the company

SIXTY

As with the Best 30, the Best 60 became a Caterpillar model in April 1925. The Caterpillar Sixty continued to be built in San Leandro (S.N. ending with A), with Peoria production commencing in late 1925 (S.N. prefix PA). This San Leandro–built 1926 vintage Sixty (S.N. 3331A) is considered one of the finest examples of this tractor type in the world today. Owner: Dave Smith. *ECO*

gradually replaced the entire tractor line that had carried over from Holt and Best and had established Caterpillar Tractor Company as the market leader. Existing models, even those that had sold thousands of units and were the envy of competition, were continually replaced with more modern designs. This progressive policy was intended to ensure that Caterpillar tractors remained the industry leaders.

In 1927 the Caterpillar Twenty was launched as the first of a new series of tractors. It was also the first machine to be designed entirely by the Caterpillar Tractor Company, and not derived from any former Best or Holt models. The Twenty looked much different from its predecessors. Gone was the open engine style of old. In its place modern sheet metal formed a sleek hood, with louvered panels covering the sides of the engine, rather like the earlier Holt models. The operator's seat area also received substantial sheet metal on its back and sides. This design turned out to be the forerunner of a new era in tractor style.

The engineering department from the former Best company had a strong hand in the Twenty's design, and it was initially built in the San Leandro plant. The Twenty was powered by an overhead-valve, four-cylinder Caterpillar 4x5-1/2-inch bore-and-stroke gasoline engine rated at 28.03-drawbar horsepower and 31.16-belt horsepower. The gearbox provided three forward speeds of 1.8, 2.6, and 3.6 miles per hour. To increase production of this model, the company set up a production line in the Peoria plant the year following its launch. The tractors from both plants were identical, but to distinguish their origin, the Peoria machines were designated with a PL serial number prefix, while those from San Leandro were given an L prefix. Two track gauges were offered, 42-inch and 55-inch. The Twenty featured long fenders that ran from the fuel tank, past the operator, and then curved downward over the rear tracks. The word TWENTY was cast on the sides of the radiator, and the usual wavy "Caterpillar" logo appeared on the front. The lettering was highlighted in crimson red. Production at the San Leandro plant would end in late 1929 with 1,970 units. In Peoria, a further 6,331 units were built until late 1932, when this first-series Twenty was replaced with the Twenty-Five tractor. The Twenty Five, and an entirely different model Twenty tractor, released in 1932, are described later.

In late 1928, Caterpillar officially released the model Ten (PT-series). First pre-viewed on September 1, 1928, Caterpillar ads announced, "a smaller size of the Caterpillar tractor . . . eagerly awaited by all small power users." Rated even smaller than the 2-Ton, its engine was a side-valve, four-cylinder 3-3/8x4-inch bore-and-stroke gasoline engine rated at 15.15-drawbar horsepower and 18.72-belt horsepower. Its three-speed gearbox provided a first gear speed of 2 miles per hour, higher than most preceding tractors. Second and third gears gave speeds of 2.6 miles per hour and 3.5 miles per hour. At 4,420 pounds (compared with the 2-ton's 5,300 pounds), the Ten was Caterpillar's smallest-ever tractor. It followed closely the design of the model Twenty introduced a year earlier, and was well received by the farming community. Its small dimensions were useful in orchards, where it could work between closely planted groves of trees. Buyers could choose between a narrow 37-inch track gauge and or a wider 44-inch gauge.

A high-clearance model was also offered for row crop work. This tractor employed an ingenious arrangement in the final drive, where an additional spur gear set provided the extra height. The bevel gear was then driven from the opposite side of the bevel pinion so that the correct rotation was maintained at the drive sprockets. A little quirk on the Ten was its gas tank position on top of the engine.

SIXTY
The Caterpillar Sixty was powered by a big four-cylinder 6-1/2x8-1/2-inch bore-and-stroke, valve-in-head gasoline motor. Depending on customer preference, the fuel tank could be ordered mounted on the right side of the tractor, or in this case, the left side. Owner: Dave Smith. *ECO*

Users reported that on hot days, vapor locks would occur in the fuel line arresting flow to the carburetor. Apparently the root of the problem was the vaporization of the over-heated gasoline in the tank. The Caterpillar Ten remained in the production line until 1933, by which time 4,932 units had left the Peoria plant.

Introduced in late 1928, the first-series Caterpillar Fifteen (PV-series) filled the gap between the Ten and Twenty tractors in power and weight. It carried a Caterpillar 3-3/4x5-inch bore-and-stroke gas engine rated at 22.77-drawbar horsepower and 25.94-belt horsepower at 1,250 rpm. Of similar design to the Ten and Twenty, the three-speed gearbox furnished speed ranges almost identical to the model Ten. The Fifteen PV-series track gauge widths were either 40 inches or 50 inches, and a high-clearance version was offered in kit form. The tractor's shipping weight was listed as 5,790 pounds. This tractor sold very well, and chalked up 7,559 sales by the time the model ceased in 1932.

In that same year, two more Caterpillar Fifteen models were introduced. These were known as the "Little" or "Small" Fifteen (7C-series), and the Fifteen "High-Clearance"

(1D-series). These two models were not intended to replace the Fifteen PV-series model. They were new tractors designed to take over the market vacated by the recently discontinued Caterpillar Ten. Both models were equipped with a Caterpillar 3-3/8x4-inch bore-and-stroke engine rated at 18.03-drawbar horsepower and 21.63-belt horsepower. Both of these models sported a three-speed gearbox that provided exactly the same speeds as the former model Ten. The High-Clearance 1D tractor was built with a 44-inch track gauge, while the 7C model offered both the 44-inch and a narrow 37-inch gauge, the same as the former Ten model.

The shortcomings of the earlier Ten were rectified in the new Fifteen tractors. These included relocation of the fuel tank from on top of to behind the engine. But the popularity of crawler tractors of this size was already waning. Farmers and other customers wanted more power than the Fifteen could offer, and both models were withdrawn from production the year after they were introduced. Only 307 of the Little Fifteen (7C) and 95 of the High-Clearance Fifteen (1D) tractors left the factory, making these models very rare today and greatly sought after by enthusiasts.

SIXTY

The Caterpillar Sixty was also available in a "Snow Special," which consisted of the same options found on the Best 60 configured for working in snow. This Sixty is shown equipped with special skeleton track shoes designed for riding over snow and ice. The opening in the shoes allows the sprocket to force out snow that might otherwise freeze up the track assembly. *ECO Collection*

In 1932, Caterpillar launched the "Small" Twenty (8C-series) as the replacement for the Fifteen (PV-series) that was discontinued the same year. The new tractor was similar in size to its forerunner, carrying the same 40-inch and 50-inch gauge options and the same three-speed gearbox. But the tractor was redesigned to overcome some shortfalls in the replaced model. The "Small" Twenty featured new sheet metal and an improved seating area. Relocating the fuel tank behind the engine allowed a lower hood and a more modern appearance. Although the same bore-and-stroke engine carried forward from the Fifteen (PV) to the Twenty (8C) tractors, its power increased slightly to 23.69-drawbar horsepower and 28.39-belt horsepower. These changes resulted in a more efficient and reliable tractor, but even these improvements failed to attract customers in the large numbers that Caterpillar had hoped for, and the Small Twenty was discontinued in 1933. The Great Depression had a lot to do with weak sales, as all industry

SIXTY

The Caterpillar Sixty, along with the Best 60, is considered one of the finest agricultural crawler tractors ever designed for its time. It sold in large numbers, and is always the centerpiece of a tractor collection in restored condition. In all there were 5,415 Best 60/Cat Sixty tractors built in San Leandro between 1919 and 1930. An additional 13,516 Cat Sixtys were produced in Peoria from 1925 through 1931, including one listed as being built in 1932. This is a San Leandro–built 1929 vintage Caterpillar Sixty (S.N. 5089A). Owner: Doug Veerkamp. *ECO*

SIXTY DIESEL ENGINE CONVERSION
In 1933, Caterpillar offered a diesel-engine conversion unit for the gasoline-powered Sixty tractor. The engine, the Cat D7700, normally found in the Diesel Fifty, was a four-cylinder 5-1/4x8-inch bore-and-stroke engine, rated at 63-brake horsepower. In 1935 the Cat D8800 (5-3/4x8-inch bore-and-stroke) diesel replaced the D7700 offering. The conversion itself took approximately 16 to 20 manhours to complete for a reasonably trained mechanic with all tools at hand. This diesel-conversion could be performed on San Leandro–built tractors with the serial numbers 2201A and up, and Peoria units PA1 and up. Only 55 of the D7700 (S.N. 5E1501) and 55 of the D8800 (S.N. 5E 6001) conversion units were produced. Records do not indicate just how many of these diesel units were actually installed in the Best 60/Cat Sixty tractors themselves. *ECO Collection*

slowed or stagnated completely. To compound matters, the Great Plains were going through a severe drought, leaving farmers with no capital to spend on new equipment. In light of these hardships, the fact that Caterpillar sold 652 of the 8C series Twenty tractors was nothing of which to be ashamed.

Almost immediately after Caterpillar brought out its model Twenty-Two (2F-series) to replace the Twenty (8C-series) in 1934, the economy quickened the pace and sales flourished. Caterpillar's persistence in marketing a small gasoline tractor was finally rewarded. The Twenty-Two, weighing 6,210 pounds, proved to be a very good seller for the company. It utilized a four-cylinder Caterpillar

4x5-inch bore-and-stroke engine rated at 25.77-drawbar horsepower and 31.54-belt-horsepower. Its improved design and nimble operation resulted in a very reliable tractor, which was well accepted in all market sectors.

As with most of its small tractors, Caterpillar offered special versions of the Twenty-Two. The "orchard special" came with the familiar low-slung seat at the rear, but it also sported large streamlined fenders that covered the upper half of each crawler with curved sheet metal. The only projection on top of the hood was a small air cleaner intake vent, and even this was treated to a streamlined cowling. Not intended for tractor aesthetics, these modern-looking curves enabled the tractor to slide under low-hanging

CHOOSING CATERPILLAR YELLOW

Before the Caterpillar merger, Best tractors were painted black with gold and red highlighting. After the merger, Caterpillar adopted Holt's colors of gray with red highlighting for the entire tractor range. These colors were not particularly striking, but customers had become used to them. Dark colors had been the tradition since tractors were invented. Just after the Great Depression, when tractor sales plummeted, someone from Caterpillar's marketing department asked, "Why not paint our tractors in bright colors?—after all we are trying to get out of the depression." A brighter color had practical advantages, too. The dingy gray was difficult to spot across a field at dusk, and not very visible on highway jobs where the machines were in danger of being hit by other vehicles. In addition, some states like Missouri and Kansas specified silver and orange, and were willing to pay a little extra for the nonstandard paint.

Convinced that a change had benefits, the company formed a committee to determine a new color scheme. Each of three Caterpillar Thirtys was painted a different color to give each choice its full effect. One was painted deep orange with a black engine, one with aluminum paint, and the third bright yellow. The committee deliberated at length before making the final choice. Initially, the committee chose the deep orange and black tractor, but the manufacturing department did not like it—they had a strong say in most company decisions at that time. Silver was the second choice, but it posed some practical and procurement problems. So the third choice, yellow, won by default. The company circulated an official memo saying that beginning December 7, 1931, all Caterpillar products shipped would be painted in Hi-Way Yellow with trademarks and trimmings in black.

The color change was not readily accepted by all. More than one dealer wrote to the company saying that their customers were not "yellow" and were not going to sit on yellow machines! Some dealers specified their next few orders painted in the old colors, and they paid the extra charge. Over the next 12 months or so, just to prove "the customer is always right," Caterpillar offered the old gray and red as an option for the more traditional customer who could not accept the new livery. But over the years, the yellow gradually became known as "Caterpillar Yellow," and was adopted by the Air Force and most highway departments. By the 1970s most other construction equipment makers were using yellow as a standard color.

TWENTY
The original Caterpillar Twenty tractor (S.N. prefix L) was produced in the San Leandro plant from 1927 through 1929. The Peoria-built Twenty (S.N. prefix PL) was in production from 1928 to 1932. The Twenty was powered by a four-cylinder 4x5-1/2-inch bore-and-stroke, overhead valve gasoline engine, and was available with a standard 42-inch track gauge and a 55-inch wide-gauge layout. Production of San Leandro Twentys amounted to 1,970 tractors, while Peoria pumped out a far greater 6,331 units. Pictured is a 1929 vintage Twenty carrying serial No. L1970. This historic tractor was the last Twenty built at the San Leandro facilities. Owner: Howard Bowers. *ECO*

branches without tangling them up in the crawler mechanism and damaging the trees. The Twenty-Two was also offered in a high-clearance version for row crop work, maintaining the 40-inch and 50-inch track gauge options.

The Twenty-Two 1J series superseded the 2F-series in 1937 but the tractor remained almost unchanged. The revised serial number prefix primarily identified an improved manufacturing process in the plant. The successful Twenty-Two tractor would continue production for a further two years until manufacture finally ended in 1939. Total sales of the 2F-series amounted to 9,999 units, with a further 5,157 sales of the latter 1J-series tractor.

Caterpillar released the Twenty-Five (3C-series) tractor in December 1931 as a replacement for the model Twenty (PL-series). Its introduction coincided with a landmark in the history of the Caterpillar company: the change in product color from the traditional gray with red highlighting to "Hi-Way Yellow" with black highlighting. The company announced the color change, along with a new Caterpillar logo to replace the wavy or "crawling" design, in December 1931. The 3C-series Twenty-Five was very similar in specification to the Twenty

TEN
The Caterpillar Ten (S.N. prefix PT) was first introduced in 1928, and stayed in production until early 1933 (three built in 1933). The Ten was powered by a Cat four-cylinder 3-3/8x4-inch bore-and-stroke L-head (Ricardo type) gasoline engine, with a three-speed transmission. The model was available in 37-inch narrow track gauge and 44-inch wide-gauge configurations. The Ten pictured is a 1929 narrow-gauge model, serial No. PT1927. Owner: Ron Miller. *ECO*

TEN "ORCHARD"
The Caterpillar Ten could be ordered with an "orchard" tailseat at no extra charge, instead of the high-mounted configuration. This Ten is a 1932 wide-gauge model, serial No. PT4787, and is equipped with front-mounted check-breakers, which push through cross ridges made for irrigation purposes in orchards or vineyards. *ECO*

TEN "ORCHARD"

The "orchard" tailseat option on the Caterpillar Ten lowered the seat by 9 inches, enabling the operator and tractor to slide under low-hanging branches. This seat configuration was also ideal in job applications where the operator needed to make frequent dismounts of the tractor during the working day. *ECO*

TEN

The Caterpillar Ten might have been small in stature, but proved to be a fairly popular tractor with some 4,932 examples built. This Ten is a 1928 model, serial No. PT-4, and is equipped with optional Bishop citrus fenders, which helped keep fruits from being bruised by the tracks as the tractor passed under low-hanging branches. *ECO*

TEN HIGH-CLEARANCE

For cultivating and other row crop work, Caterpillar offered the Ten in a 44-inch wide-gauge "high-clearance" configuration. The drawbar on this model could also be easily removed for additional ground clearance when needed. Only 395 of the high-clearance Tens were produced. This 1930 HC Ten carries serial No. PT3923. *ECO*

TEN HIGH-CLEARANCE
The Caterpillar Ten "high-clearance" could be equipped with various factory extras, such as a canopy, an enclosed cab, auxiliary fuel tank, front pull hook, stationary drive unit, and rear power take-off. This HC Ten from April 1933 is a special factory build for the U.S. Forestry Service, equipped with a reinforced grille guard, lighting system, and exhaust spark arrester. *ECO Collection*

(PL-series) it replaced, with track gauges, speeds, and engine remaining the same. The advertised engine power showed a slight increase to 28.63-drawbar horsepower and 35.18-belt horsepower. But this increase was due to a change in how the power ratings were measured, rather than an actual increase in engine power. Shipping weight for the Twenty Five was 7,707 pounds.

When the Twenty Five was announced, a number of the former Twenty (PL) tractors still sat unsold in the Peoria yard. According to some retired company executives,

TEN HIGH-CLEARANCE
This unique 1930 Caterpillar Ten "high-clearance" (S.N. PT4165) is equipped with a factory original Caterpillar-designed mower (S.N. 4C33), which is one of only 175 ever produced. This Ten was factory ordered with the mower attachment, as well as a special yellow paint scheme instead of the standard gray, most likely for roadside maintenance mowing requirements. It's not yet clear whether this special factory paint request was originally trimmed in red or black, if at all. Until that question is answered, the restoration stays as is. The Cat mower option was also available for the Fifteen tractor. Owner: Patrick J. Eder. *ECO*

FIFTEEN AND "SMALL" FIFTEEN
Caterpillar produced two different standard model types of its Fifteen series tractors. The oldest was the model Fifteen (S.N. prefix PV), originally introduced in late 1928, and in production until 1932, with 7,559 built. The other model was referred to as the "Little" or "Small" Fifteen (S.N. prefix 7C), which was produced from 1932 to 1933, totaling some 307 units. Pictured is a 1929 Fifteen (S.N. PV2491) on the left, and a 1933 "Small" Fifteen (S.N. 7C271) on the right. Originally, this vintage Fifteen PV-series tractor would have been painted gray, but the owner preferred the brighter Hi-Way Yellow for its restoration. *ECO*

the company decided to change their serial numbers and radiator sides to conform to the new Twenty-Five nomenclature, rather than selling them off as old inventory. This change was possible because the two models were so similar. The change went unnoticed by all except the most discerning customer, but the keen eye could notice that the wavy or crawling Caterpillar logo remained unchanged on the front of the radiator top, and this clue identified a Twenty-Five (3C) as one of the tractors changed from the former Twenty (PL) series. Records show that a total of 638 Twenty-Five (3C) tractors were sold, including those converted from former Twenty (PL) units.

Less than two years after introducing the Twenty-Five, Caterpillar replaced it with a redesigned and improved model, the Twenty-Eight (4F-series) with a listed shipping weight of 7,830 pounds. A new engine boosted power to 30.49-drawbar horsepower and 37.47-belt horsepower. The four-cylinder gasoline engine had a 4-3/16x5-1/2-inch bore and stroke. The 42-inch and 52-inch track gauge options continued, and so did the three speeds from 1.8 to 3.6 miles per hour. The Twenty-Eight was a very well-designed tractor,

FIFTEEN "ORCHARD"
The Caterpillar Fifteen PV-series could also be ordered equipped with a tailseat configuration for orchard and vineyard work. The PV-series Fifteen was powered by a four-cylinder, 3-3/4x5-inch bore-and-stroke, gasoline engine. It was available in 40-inch narrow-gauge and 50-inch wide-gauge track layouts. *ECO Collection*

FIFTEEN HIGH-CLEARANCE
The Caterpillar Fifteen High-Clearance (S.N. prefix 1D) was introduced at the same time as the "Small" Fifteen 7C-series. While the 7C-series Fifteen was available in track gauges of 37 and 44 inches, the 1D-series only was available with the 44-inch wide-gauge setup. The same four-cylinder 3-3/8x4-inch bore-and-stroke gasoline engine powered both tractor models. Only 95 examples of the Fifteen High-Clearance were ever built. Pictured is an extremely rare 1932 vintage Fifteen HC, carrying serial No. 1D11. *ECO*

TWENTY "ORCHARD"
The Caterpillar "Small" Twenty 8C-series could be ordered in a tailseat configuration for orchard and nursery work. The 8C-series Twenty was available in 40-inch narrow gauge and 50-inch wide-gauge track layouts. This 1933 vintage Twenty (S.N. 8C617) is a narrow-gauge model. Production would end on this model series in 1933 with some 652 tractors being built. *ECO*

and management was disappointed with sales of only 1,171 units. The company therefore ceased production in late 1935. The slow sales were probably attributable to the diesel-powered tractors, with their lower operating costs, just coming onto the market. As we shall see in the next chapter, diesel power would not only dominate the market for the largest tractors, it would influence all tractor markets.

But the gasoline tractor was not dead, and to prove it Caterpillar launched the first three of a new line of gas tractors in 1934. These were the R-2, R-3, and R-5, and they got their start in a substantial government order for tractors different from those in Caterpillar's lineup. These tractors were purchased for work on President Roosevelt 's "New Deal" construction projects, and the 'R' designation commemorated the president's name. The New Deal created agencies to manage new construction and rural conservation projects of all kinds. These agencies included the Tennessee Valley Authority (TVA), which provided power for rural electrification, initially from dams and hydroelectric stations it built at strategic locations. These dams also provided means for flood control. The Civilian Conservation Corps (CCC) transformed huge tracts of

TWENTY
Caterpillar introduced the "Small" Twenty (S.N. prefix 8C) in 1932 as the replacement for the PV-series Fifteen. It was powered by a four-cylinder 3-3/4x5-inch bore-and-stroke flathead gasoline engine. This "Small" Twenty is a wide-gauge 1932 model (S.N. 8C244) with optional canopy top. *ECO*

TWENTY-TWO

The Caterpillar Twenty-Two was a very popular tractor in the marketplace. The Twenty-Two was built in two model series: the 2F-series from 1934 to 1937 (9,999 built), and the 1J-series from 1937 to 1939 (5,157 built). The Twenty-Two was the replacement for the "Small" Twenty 8C-series. Here is a vintage 1937 model Twenty-Two (1J1507). Owner Marv Fery. *ECO*

TWENTY-TWO "ORCHARD"

On most of Caterpillar's smaller tractors of this time period, a tailseat option was offered at no extra cost for orchard and nursery work. All Twenty-Two crawlers were powered by a four-cylinder 4x5-inch bore-and-stroke gasoline engine. Two track gauges were offered: a 40-inch narrow-gauge and a 50-inch-wide gauge configuration. This "orchard" wide-gauge Twenty-Two is a 1934 model, carrying serial No. 2F1321 SP. *ECO*

TWENTY-TWO "ORCHARD"

The tailseat version of the Caterpillar Twenty-Two could also be equipped with a snazzy set of orchard fenders, which protected low-hanging fruit tree branches from damage as the tractor worked around them. This fender option was available for the regular high-mounted tractor seat as well. This immaculate tractor is a 1935 orchard Twenty-Two (S.N. 2F4200W). Owner: Larry Maasdam. *ECO*

TWENTY-TWO HIGH-CLEARANCE

Rarest of the Caterpillar Twenty-Two tractors was the limited production "high-clearance" configuration for cultivating and row crop work. Pictured is an ultra-rare 1936 vintage high-clearance model, carrying serial No. 2F8505H SP. Owners: Dan Plote and Bob LaVoie. *ECO*

TWENTY-TWO HIGH-CLEARANCE

The Caterpillar Twenty-Two "high-clearance" configuration is so rare that this 1936 2F-series tractor is the only known restored example in the world at the time of this writing (outside of one or two incomplete "parts" machines). Owners: Dan Plote and Bob LaVoie. *ECO*

TWENTY-FIVE "ORCHARD"

The Caterpillar Twenty-Five (S.N. prefix 3C) was first introduced in December 1931 as the replacement for the PL-series Twenty model line. It was in production until 1933, with just 638 units built. Pictured is a 1931 "orchard" tailseat, wide-gauge Twenty-Five (3C111). Because of the "wavy" Caterpillar logo on the front radiator, and low serial number, this tractor is very likely one of the factory-converted Twenty PL-series units re-manufactured from existing inventory. *ECO*

TWENTY-FIVE
The Caterpillar Twenty-Five was powered by a four-cylinder 4x5-1/2-inch bore-and-stroke gasoline engine. Available track gauges were a 42-inch narrow-gauge and a 55-inch wide-gauge. This rare wide-gauge 1931 vintage Twenty-Five (S.N. 3C168) is equipped with optional 18-inch "swamp" angle steel track shoes and electric lighting system. Owner: Keith Clark. *ECO*

TWENTY-EIGHT
Caterpillar replaced the short-lived model Twenty-Five with the Twenty-Eight (S.N. prefix 4F) in late 1933. It was equipped with a four-cylinder 4-3/16x5-1/2-inch bore-and-stroke gasoline engine. Track gauges offered were the same as the Twenty-Five. Production ceased on this model in 1935, with approximately 1,171 tractors built. Pictured is a 1935 vintage, wide-gauge Twenty-Eight (S.N. 4F929 SP), with optional electric start. Owner: Marv Fery. *ECO*

THIRTY

The Caterpillar Thirty series 6G was first introduced in late 1935. It was powered by a four-cylinder 4-1/4x5-1/2-inch bore-and-stroke gasoline engine, and was available in 44-inch narrow-gauge and 60-inch wide-gauge track layouts. This tractor model would be re-designated the R-4 in 1938. Both models were virtually the same except for the elimination of an upper track roller on the R-4. *Courtesy Caterpillar, Inc. Corporate Archives*

barren land into productive forests by planting millions of seedling trees and constructing roads and bridges to access these lands. The Works Progress Administration (WPA) was assigned the responsibility to develop parks and build extensive transportation facilities including roads, docks, and airports. These projects gave the economy a much-needed boost and reduced unemployment. They also provided Caterpillar with huge sales.

After completing the government orders, Caterpillar retained the R-series designation for all subsequent gasoline tractor models. This change was necessary because customers were becoming confused over the old spelled-out numbers on the tractor models. The model number no longer referred to the tractor horsepower, and as more power was advertised in the same model, it was still referred to by the same model number. And as new models were coming out with the same horsepower as a previous model, a different model number was needed. The new model designation made the tractor salesman's life a lot easier. In the case of the diesel models, discussed

R-2

The Caterpillar R-2 was produced in three model series. The 5E3501-series (40- and 50-inch track gauges) was built from late 1934 to 1937. It was powered by a four-cylinder 4x5-inch bore-and-stroke engine. In 1938 the 4J-series (40-inch gauge) and 6J-series (50-inch gauge) models were introduced, whose chassis were based on the D2. The 4J- and 6J-series were both powered by the same four-cylinder Cat 3400G, 3-3/4x5-inch bore-and-stroke motor. Pictured is a 1939 vintage R-2 (S.N. 4J672 SP) with optional citrus fenders. *ECO*

R-4

The Caterpillar 6G-series Thirty became the 6G-series R-4 in 1938. About the only noticeable change to the tractor line, other than the badging, was that the Thirty utilized two upper track rollers, and the R-4 only used one. This R-4 is shown with optional "orchard" fenders. *ECO Collection*

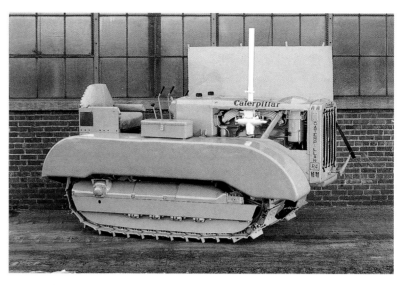

R-3
Produced from 1934 to 1935 only, the Caterpillar R-3 (S.N. prefix 5E2501) is considered a very rare tractor. Of the 60 produced in total, only a couple of restored units are known to exist today. The R-3 was powered by a four-cylinder Cat 5500G, 4-1/2x5-1/2-inch bore-and-stroke gasoline engine, and was available in a 55-inch wide-gauge track configuration only. Pictured is a prized early 1935 vintage R-3, carrying serial No. 5E2532 SP. Owner: Tyler family. *ECO*

R-5
The Caterpillar R-5 was first introduced in 1934 (starting S.N. 5E3001). It was replaced by the 4H-series (starting S.N. 4H501) in 1936. The last model produced was the 3R-series from 1940, which was built in that year only. All were powered by the four-cylinder Cat 7500G, 5-1/2x6-1/2-inch bore-and-stroke gasoline engine, and were offered in 56-inch narrow-gauge and 74-inch wide-gauge track configurations. *ECO Collection*

in the next chapter, a 'D' was added behind the R for a while, but in late 1937 the R was dropped, leaving D for diesel and R for gasoline tractors.

The R-2 was basically derived from the Twenty-Two model. The first series began with serial No. 5E3501, and utilized a Caterpillar four-cylinder 4x5-inch bore-and-stroke engine rated at 28.2-drawbar horsepower and 32.1-belt horsepower. However, very few of the 5E series R-2 tractors were built over its 2-1/2-year production life. In fact records show shipments of only 83 units. In 1938 two more versions of the R-2 came out, the 4J and 6J series, with 40-inch and 50-inch track gauges, respectively. These two models were powered by a Caterpillar 3400G four-cylinder 3-3/4x5-inch bore-and-stroke engine rated at 25.5-drawbar

horsepower and 31.5 belt horsepower. Production of these models ran until 1942, by which time 1,185 of the 4J series and 1,150 of the 6J had been manufactured.

The first R-3 gasoline tractor, serial No. 5E2501, was produced in 1934. This tractor was similar to the Caterpillar Twenty-eight, but boasted the more-powerful 5500G four-cylinder engine with 4-1/2x5-1/2-inch bore and stroke, rated at 36.64-drawbar horsepower and 43.88-belt horsepower. A rare tractor indeed, the R-3 managed a sales count of only 60 units.

The last of the trio of R-series gasoline tractors released in 1934 was the R-5, of which three different series were produced. Approximately 40 of the first series were based on the model Thirty Five, which had been introduced in 1932

R-6

The rarest of all Caterpillar Tractor Company crawlers is the elusive R-6 from 1941. The R-6 was essentially a D6 tractor chassis equipped with a gasoline-powered Cat 4600G, six-cylinder 4-1/4x5-1/2-inch bore-and-stroke engine, and was available in 60- and 74-inch track gauges. Even though a handful of tractors were said to have been built and shipped in 1941, not one example is known to exist in the world today. Even the serial number prefix code is not known, since all records of this tractor are missing from Caterpillar's archives. *Courtesy Caterpillar, Inc. Corporate Archives*

and carried the same gas engine as the current Fifty, a 50-drawbar horsepower model released in 1931 (see Chapter 5). These were given serial numbers starting with 5E3001. Subsequent tractors in the 5E-series were based on the Forty model, which replaced the Thirty Five in 1934. In 1936, Caterpillar presented a new series of R-5 tractors starting with serial No. 4H501. Production count for the 5E and 4H models were 500 and 1,000 units, respectively. Finally, another 49 R-5 tractors were assembled in 1940 and shipped with serial number prefix 3R.

The R-2, R-3, and R-5 tractors ordered by the government incorporated arrangements slightly different from standard. For example, the steering levers on the R-5 government tractors operated both the steering clutches and brakes, and the main clutch was operated by a foot pedal. This arrangement appeared to be a breakthrough

leading to a more simple method of tractor operation, but it was not generally adopted by Caterpillar for its other models. Even with orders boosted by the government, Caterpillar considered production numbers of these small gasoline tractors disappointing. The low sales indicated that the diesel-powered tractor was surely taking over the market, even for the small crawler tractor.

One bright spark was the model R-4 gasoline tractor. Originally launched by Caterpillar in 1935 as the Thirty (6G-series), it was a totally new design bearing no resemblance to the earlier Thirty (PS-series), which was discontinued in 1932. The new model utilized a four-cylinder Caterpillar 4-1/4x5-1/2-inch bore-and-stroke gasoline engine rated at 35-drawbar horsepower and 41-belt horsepower, and incorporated new features that would be retained in many subsequent tractors. In 1938 the Thirty

(6G-series) was renamed the R-4 to bring its nomenclature in line with the rest of Caterpillar's tractor line. At that point, the only remaining tractor with the old nomenclature was the Twenty-Two, but that model was retired the following year. R-4 production continued throughout World War II up to 1944, by which time 5,383 units had been produced. The R-4 turned out to be the last of the gasoline-powered tractors offered commercially by Caterpillar.

Probably the rarest of Caterpillar's gasoline tractors is the R-6. Built in 1941, it was based on a D-6 chassis and offered with a standard 60-inch or optional 74-inch track gauge. The R-6 used a Caterpillar 4600G six-cylinder engine with 4-1/4x5-1/2-inch bore and stroke, developing 55-drawbar horsepower and 65-belt horsepower. Very little information survives on this rare model, as it was released the same year America went to war with Japan. At that time, Caterpillar removed much of its records and archives to offsite locations for security reasons, in compliance with government requests that companies' records be decentralized. But in these locations, the records were not as secure as they should have been, and some were never returned to their original locations after the war. It is believed that no more than five R-6 tractors were produced and there are no known surviving examples.

Throughout the 1930s, Caterpillar strongly promoted its tractors for agricultural use, even though we will see later that the company also broadened into the construction and earthmoving markets during this period. Ease of operation and maintenance were the major selling points directed at the farming community. Caterpillar literature of the day extolled the tractor's simplified design:

Needless parts are eliminated! Essential parts have the reserve strength far above full-load operating requirements. Caterpillar uses bearings of the size and type to minimize friction, and provide sturdy support for moving parts - features that save time and upkeep. A 1930s brochure claimed, "Many young people from 10 years old, and up, are operating Caterpillar tractors. Field results prove that the operator does not need special skill or training to drive and maintain the Caterpillar tractor successfully. That indicates how simple and reliable Caterpillar tractors are."

Even as it stressed the simplicity of its machines, Caterpillar was determined to keep its designs fresh and technologically advanced. Despite the Great Depression, Caterpillar introduced some successful and important designs in the 1930s, doing as much as it could with gasoline power. But a different type of fuel was starting to dominate the heavy machine industry, and Caterpillar would become a leader in this technology as well.

Old Tusko

CHAPTER FOUR

EARLY DIESEL POWER

Sales of gasoline-powered tractors began to dwindle in the 1930s for two main reasons. First, the Great Depression had cast a blanket of uncertainty over the entire agricultural and industrial world. Farmers had little or no money for capital expenditures, so tractor sales suffered in all markets. Second was the increasing popularity of diesel-powered machinery, a trend Caterpillar's own machines had helped foster. Diesel was a cheaper fuel, and diesel engines had excellent torque for performing heavy work. The market's gradual changeover from gasoline to diesel tractors took place almost entirely during the 1930s. Caterpillar introduced its first diesel tractor in 1931. Ten years later, Caterpillar's gasoline tractor line was almost extinct with only the two small R-2 and R-4 models continuing any significant sales into the early 1940s.

The diesel engine was not new when Caterpillar launched its first diesel tractor, but the company played a major part in developing its use in mobile equipment. German native Rudolph Diesel invented the engine that carried his name. Diesel published a research paper in 1893, for which he was awarded a German patent for his design theory for a high-compression, sparkless engine. The first prototype diesel engine was operational by 1895, and two years later Diesel sold several manufacturing licenses to entrepreneurs. Among these licensees was Adolphus Busch, a wealthy brewer

Diesel Sixty
The engine in the Diesel Sixty was the Cat D9900, four-cylinder, 61/8x9 1/4-inch bore and stroke, valve-in-head diesel engine, originally rated at 63 drawbar and 73 belt horsepower. Transmission was a three speed forward and one reverse unit Only a 72-inch track-gauge configuration was offered. Owner: Allen F. Anderson. *ECO*

DIESEL SIXTY PROTOTYPE
This Caterpillar tractor was one of the factory prototype test mules fabricated around 1930 to put some real field time on the newly designed D9900 diesel engine. It is mounted in a gas Cat Sixty chassis equipped with a custom-built radiator. Note the mounting bracket supports for the starting pony motor. These brackets, along with many details of the pony motor itself, were not yet to production standards and would change before the design would officially go into production. *ECO Collection*

DIESEL SIXTY
This is one of the earliest images taken of the first production Caterpillar Diesel Sixty tractor (S.N. 1C1) in the summer of 1931. Compare the mounting supports of the pony motor, which are now part of the castings, to that of the prototype pilot unit from 1930. When comparing the two, most of the changes centered around the pony motor area. Only minor alterations were made to the D9900 Diesel itself. This tractor would ship from the San Leandro plant in September 1931, but would not be officially sold until November. Only Diesel Sixty tractors 1C1 and 1C2 were built in San Leandro with the "crawly" Caterpillar logo, and both were painted gray with no color trim. The remaining machines were produced in Peoria and painted Hi-Way Yellow, trimmed in black, except 1C3, which is also believed to have been shipped gray with no color trim. *courtesy of Caterpillar, Inc. Corporate Archives*

DIESEL SIXTY
This image of the Caterpillar Diesel Sixty "Tusko" (the "Old" was added some years later) was taken in April 1956 with its then owner, Harold W. Hartfield of Arlington, Oregon, looking on. Mr. Hartfield was the uncle of the present owner of the tractor, Allen F. Anderson. *Anderson Collection*

from St. Louis, Missouri. In 1898, Busch began producing the first diesel engine in the United States.

Another American, George A. Dow, a pump manufacturer from Alameda, California, became very interested in making the diesel engine himself. He made several trips to England to meet with Diesel, who was setting up a new engine factory in Ipswich. Following Diesel's untimely death at sea in 1915, Dow succeeded in obtaining manufacturing rights from the British makers in Ipswich.

Dow was an old schoolmate of C.L. Best and the latter kept in close contact with the diesel engine's progress over the years leading up to the Holt and Best merger. In fact, both companies had observed the diesel's application and considered installing the new engine in their tractors. But early diesels, bulky and heavy, were more suited for marine and stationary applications. In the latter case, they were usually located on a firm concrete slab, often inside a building. Here, compactness was not an issue and maintenance could be carried out in relatively clean conditions. Such stationary engines operated at

constant speed under uniform load. A tractor's engine, however, operates at varying speeds in outdoor conditions that can be quite harsh to say the least.

An experiment with diesel power proved the early engines were not up to the task. In the early 1920s, contractor Henry J. Kaiser installed an Atlas diesel engine in a Caterpillar and a Monarch tractor. Built by John Lorimer for the Atlas Imperial Company of Oakland, California, the Atlas engine had a good reputation in stationary applications. But once on the job alongside the Mississippi River, the bulky engines added too much weight, and just about destroyed both tractors.

C.L. Best had already decided that he wanted to build diesel-powered tractors at the time of Caterpillar Tractor Company's formation. While talking with his old friend Dow in late 1925, Best learned that Dow was ready to quit the diesel business and he offered Best his chief diesel engineer, Art Rosen. As early as 1923, Rosen started writing to Pliny Holt. Later, Holt discussed the diesel's advantages with the other company directors. The weak financial condition

DIESEL SIXTY
Without a doubt, the most famous Caterpillar crawler tractor in the world today is this Diesel Sixty (S.N. 1C12), better known as "Old Tusko."
Named after a cantankerous old elephant at the Portland Zoo, this tractor set a world record for nonstop plowing in March and April of 1932.
Owner: Allen F. Anderson. *ECO*

DIESEL SIXTY
"Old Tusko" stands tall, surrounded by thousands of acres of wheat fields. During its working life of some 30 years, it put in over 70,000 operating hours in these fields. *ECO*

cultivating the soil on cotton and sugar cane plantations in this and other parts of the world. Under this system, two big steam engines equipped with horizontal winding drums and cables pulled the plow back and forth across the field while a third man rode the plow. Steam-powered tractors, built by firms such as John Fowler & Company Ltd. and J. & H. McLaren Ltd., both of Leeds, England, had captured the lion's share of this market. Holt had pursued these cable-plowing operators offering his crawler tractors as a more efficient substitute. His method required only one machine and one operator to handle the job.

The Sudan plowing demonstration was a chance for heavy equipment manufacturers to show off their rival technologies. Caterpillar sent a model Sixty to the site along with Caterpillar personnel. They had heard their competition was going to be a Fowler engine, and knowing Fowler's reputation for big, cumbersome steam tractors, the Caterpillar people were brimming with confidence. At the site, they got a shock when instead of an old steam outfit, Fowler brought a brand-new crawler tractor fitted with a Benz diesel engine. It outshone the Sixty hands down, and easily won the competition.

Caterpillar took the demonstration results very seriously, and almost immediately ordered a Benz diesel and had it shipped to their research department for evaluation.

of the company and the pending merger of Holt with Best resulted in no decisive action. However, correspondence continued about the prospect of installing diesel engines in crawler tractors in the future.

In 1927 diesel development got a real boost from a tractor comparative demonstration in the cotton fields of the Anglo-Egyptian Sudan, Africa. Since the mid-1850s, "cable-plowing" had been the standard method of

CABLE PLOWING

Before crawler tractors came on the scene, cable plowing was one of the most widely used methods of mechanized cultivation. The method usually employed two steam traction engines positioned at opposite sides of the field to be plowed. One engine was equipped with a horizontal steam-driven winding drum, which pulled a plow across the field by a steel cable. A second cable ran from the drum across the field, through a sheave block fixed to the other tractor, and then back to the plow. With this arrangement the plow could be pulled back and forth across the field. The plow could work in both directions, as it had two sets of shares, one facing in each direction. As the plowing progressed, the traction engines moved slowly along the edges of the field. Other arrangements could be laid out, utilizing fixed or moveable anchors for the dead sheave.

English inventor John Fowler first demonstrated cable plowing in 1855. He established the Steam Plow Works at Leeds, England, in 1860. John Fowler & Company Ltd. shipped its first pair of steam plowing engines in 1862, and soon became one of the leading builders of traction engines, stationary engines, and railway locomotives in the United Kingdom. In 1887 it built the world's largest colliery winding engine, weighing 515 tons, with a 54x84-inch bore and stroke. Its conical winding drum tapered from 34 feet to 18 feet in diameter.

Starting in the 1920s, Fowler developed a line of crawler tractors sized to compete directly with Caterpillar models. In 1927 the Gyrotiller appeared, a special crawler tractor powered by a 225-horse-power Ricardo gas engine, and fitted with a rotary cultivator attachment.

DIESEL SIXTY
In its last years of service, "Old Tusko" smoked so much that many in the area mistook the hazy black cloud in the sky for a field fire. When the local fire department arrived on the scene to battle the suspected blaze, all they found was Tusko going about its duties. This same scenario would repeat itself a few more times before the tractor's retirement. In 1992, Diesel Sixty 1C12 was completely restored to like-new condition by The Halton Company, a Portland, Oregon, Caterpillar dealer. It now enjoys its well-deserved retirement years near Arlington, Oregon, the only home it has ever known. Owner: Allen F. Anderson. *ECO*

Following complete analysis of this engine and a few by other manufacturers, the Caterpillar researchers concluded that if the company was going to move forward with a reliable diesel that would maintain Caterpillar's reputation for tough tractors that thrived on rigorous site conditions out in the elements, it would have to design one of its own.

Engineer Arthur Rosen led a design team responsible for Caterpillar's first diesel engine, a four-cylinder prototype assembled for testing purposes at the San Leandro, California, plant. Management had given Rosen the following guidelines:

The new diesel engine had to 1) maintain its efficiency and run smoothly over a wide load range; 2) be easy to service and not require delicate checks and adjustments; 3) incorporate an independent starting system; and 4) contain dust-proof operating parts. Unlike the stationary diesels in common use at the time, Rosen's group needed a powerplant that would stand up to jolts, vibrations, outdoor weather, constantly variable speeds, and occasional abuse from unskilled operators. A diesel-powered vehicle is subjected to an entirely different set of demands than that of a stationary engine.

Over a number of years, Caterpillar allocated nearly all of its engineering research budget to diesel engine development. They spent over $1 million even before the first prototype was tested. Two key elements the developers had to address were fuel injection and metallurgy. The big stationary engines used a delicate method for mixing air and fuel to ensure atomization. This method worked well at fixed load and speed, but not under a tractor's variable demands. The Bosch Company in Germany had developed a variable-delivery hydraulic fuel injector that controlled the engine's speed and power. The first Caterpillar diesel tractors used the Bosch system, but

Caterpillar later perfected its own design after further research. The company also developed high-strength steels for internal engine parts, and new casting methods for cylinder heads and engine blocks to withstand the extreme pressures required in a diesel system.

The company produced a prototype followed by two full-sized diesels, each mounted in a modified Caterpillar Sixty-type crawler chassis. Following further testing and design changes, the first Caterpillar diesel tractor, the Diesel Sixty, was ready for the market in September 1931.

Compared to the gas-powered Sixty, the Diesel Sixty had a heavier reinforced frame, modified radiator, and a special lower-geared transmission. A heavy equalizer leaf spring connecting the crawler side frames replaced the previous equalizer bar. The crawler recoil springs were doubled, and the track gauge was set at 72 inches. In its early years of production, Caterpillar service staff monitored the performance of each tractor delivered. Most enjoyed busy travel schedules that took them to many parts of the world. Their feedback resulted in a number of minor improvements, all designed to enhance availability and reduce breakdowns. Steel castings in several areas replaced former fabricated or riveted components, and overall weight increased to 24,390 pounds, from 20,500 pounds for the gas tractor. But unlike modern crawler tractors, the Diesel Sixty bore almost no sheet metal, exposing the diesel engine and all its components to the elements.

The engine in Caterpillar's first diesel tractor was the D9900, with four cylinders and 6-1/8x9-1/4-inch bore and stroke. Initially, this powerplant was rated at 63-drawbar horsepower and 75-belt horsepower. By February 1932, these figures had risen to 68-drawbar horsepower and 79-belt horsepower. By the time 1C-series tractor production ceased at the end of 1932, the company listed power ratings of 70.25-drawbar horsepower and 83.86-belt horsepower at 700 rpm. To aid starting the big diesel, a two-cylinder gas pony motor was installed and used to crank the big engine through a clutch. When the tractor's main engine was running properly, the pony engine was disengaged and shut off. Caterpillar retained this method of starting diesel tractors well into the 1950s.

One of the main advantages of diesel power was its far superior low-end torque. A diesel-powered tractor possesses much greater lugging capability than a gas tractor of similar horsepower, and maximum power is available over a much wider working range. The other advantage is its superior fuel economy. The big gasoline tractors of the day consumed an enormous amount of fuel, making those with greater than 70 horsepower almost uneconomical to operate. Fuel consumption of 10 gallons per hour was normal for tractors like the Sixty, so the tractor needed a huge fuel tank if refueling was to be kept to a once-daily chore. Diesel fuel offered better economy and cost only 4 to 7 cents a gallon, compared with 14 to 16 cents per gallon for gasoline.

The first Diesel Sixty tractor was sold to the W. C. Schuder farm in Woodland, California. It was allocated serial No. 1C2 and delivered on September 14, 1931. Tractor No. 1C1 was actually the first Diesel Sixty tractor completed, but it was not sold until November 7, 1931, when it was shipped to California Equities Co., Ltd. in Stockton, California. These first two Diesel Sixty tractors were made in the San Leandro plant and were the only two of this model made at that location. They were painted in the traditional Caterpillar gray. Subsequent Diesel Sixtys and the successor model Diesel Sixty Five tractors were all produced in the East Peoria, Illinois, plant and were painted in the new Caterpillar Hi-Way Yellow, the color adopted by the company on December 7, 1931. Tractor No. 1C3 was the first Diesel Sixty to come off the production line at the East Peoria plant. It was delivered to the Oahu Sugar Company in Waupahu, Oahu, Hawaii.

The 1C-series Diesel Sixty and Diesel Sixty Five tractors were produced over a two-year period with a total of only 157 units sold. Tractors 1C1 through 1C14 were manufactured in 1931, the balance produced in 1932. The early models were designated Diesel Sixty, while the latter ones were known as Diesel Sixty Five models. Tractor enthusiasts are sometimes confused over the 1C-series designations because no serial number demarcation exists to distinguish when the change took place. Adding to the confusion, tractors produced in the middle of the production run were simply called the Caterpillar Diesel. Even the names on the radiator castings offer no clue to the exact tractor model designation. Most of the early models in 1931 had SIXTY cast on their radiator sides, but at least two are known to have carried the word DIESEL. Most, but not all, of those produced in 1932 carried the DIESEL casting.

SELLING THE DIESEL

Sales of the new diesel tractor were slow at first, but those who dared to purchase the unit were rewarded with high availability and low operating costs that exceeded expectations. One example was Diesel Sixty 1C12, sold initially to Mark V. Weatherford's Fairview Ranch in Arlington, Oregon, on February 29, 1932. This tractor made a name for itself during a test observed by four impartial judges, three of whom were agricultural engineers from Oregon State College,

Washington State College, and the University of Idaho. Going 23 hours daily, six days a week, the machine plowed 6,880 acres of Oregon soil in 46 days. The total operating cost including fuel, lubrication, and repairs amounted to only 7.78 cents per acre. Fred Lewis, a Caterpillar field engineer for the Service Department, reported on the machine's progress in his March 10, 1932, report. He stated: "All plowing is being done in third gear except for a few areas where steep pitches in the field make it necessary to shift to second gear. The engine seems to handle the load with ease, and smokes only slightly when on a steep pitch."

The event attracted much publicity as, apart from the officials, 150 observers from a half-dozen states watched the closing hours of the event on April 29, 1932. They witnessed a world record for nonstop plowing, and a startling demonstration of low-cost dieselized farming.

Tractor 1C12 was sold in 1935 to Elwood and Harold Hartfield, also of Arlington. They named it "Tusko" after

DIESEL SIXTY-FIVE
The Caterpillar Diesel Sixty-Five was still powered by the Cat D9900 diesel engine, but was rated with a bit more power at 68-drawbar, 79-belt, and 85-brake horsepower. Produced from 1931 through 1932, only 157 Diesel Sixty/Sixty-Five tractors were built. Pictured is a 1932 Diesel Sixty-Five, serial No. 1C51. Owners: Ted Halton of The Halton Co. and Dave Smith. *ECO*

factory. This would ensure that any problems could be attended to quickly. The first dozen or so were shipped with an attractive mahogany box filled with small parts that possibly might be needed at any time.

Caterpillar management had seen the advantages of diesel power well documented and were therefore surprised when the company's first diesel tractor was not a resounding sales success. The Great Depression carried part of the blame, but potential customers were also skeptical of the new technology. Money was in short supply and no one wanted to be the first to invest in something new—and in their minds, unproven. In the early 1930s, the Diesel Sixty's sales lagged behind all other Caterpillar models.

Compounding the situation were some problems with the early diesel engines, which caused much frustration for their owners. As it turned out, the fault lay with inconsistent fuel mixtures, rather than some design flaw in the tractor. In the early stages of the diesel era, the various suppliers across the nation could not produce a consistent fuel. And many farmers mistakenly believed that a diesel engine would run on just about anything combustible.

Diesel Sixty-Five
The Caterpillar Diesel Sixty-Five was still powered by the Cat D9900 diesel engine, but was rated with a bit more power at 68 drawbar, 79 belt, and 85 brake horsepower. Produced from 1931 through 1932, 157 Diesel Sixty/Sixty-Five tractors were built. Pictured is a 1932 Diesel Sixty-Five, serial number 1C51.

an elephant at the Portland Zoo. Today, known as "Old Tusko," the tractor is in the proud ownership of Allen F. Anderson, nephew of the Hartfield brothers. It is commonly regarded as the most famous Caterpillar Diesel tractor ever built.

Until all the bugs had been ironed out of the first diesel tractors, Caterpillar carefully selected the customers and locations where the tractors were to work. Management wanted to make sure the type of work would not ruin the tractor, and that the work site was near the

The view from the operator's seat of the Diesel Sixty-Five shows the clear field of vision to the right and left of the tractor. Without any sheet metal, it often seemed like you were literally riding on top of the big diesel engine itself. *ECO*

One farmer reportedly tried to run his tractor on some old road oil left on the ground after a paving job. A similar supply problem arose with lubricating oils, as there were few available that could stand up to diesel engine applications. There were engine problems everywhere—stuck piston rings, cylinder walls scored, main bearings burned up. Every diesel engine shipped had to be followed up and serviced by Caterpillar or dealer personnel.

Caterpillar recognized these fuel and lubrication problems almost immediately, and set about correcting the problem. They realized that if the diesel engine was going to be a long-term success, then appropriate lubricants and fuel of consistent quality had to be widely available. Caterpillar spearheaded research into the formulation of more consistent fuels, and shared research funding with some of the major oil producers to pioneer new lubricants more suitable for diesel applications. One such product was DELO (Diesel Engine Lubricating Oil), the first detergent, multi-compound oil. But finding distribution for the product proved a major challenge, probably because of its higher cost. The problem eased after Caterpillar began supplying the oil companies with single-cylinder diesel engines so they could develop and test lubricants that would eventually be recommended for use in Caterpillar diesels. The company also developed new high-grade fuel filters to ensure the diesels ran at peak efficiency.

Once the fuel manufacturing and distribution problems were addressed, it was then up to the customer to store and handle the fuel properly. Caterpillar published several booklets giving advice on fuel cleanliness, and trade publications also picked up the issue. The following extract appeared in *National Petroleum News*, and was repeated in Caterpillar's publication, *Clean Fuel*:

Perhaps the most prolific source of trouble in diesel engines is the use of dirty fuels, and by this is meant the introduction of solid matter after shipment from the refiner. By far, the greatest cause of this contamination is the careless handling in the field. This applies particularly to field distribution of fuel for tractor and automotive engines, and it is in these particular engines that cleanliness is of the most vital importance. Since diesel fuel is heavier and more viscous than gasoline, it will hold dirt in suspension for longer periods of time, and therefore greater care must be taken with diesel fuel than with gasoline.

DIESEL SIXTY-FIVE
The Diesel Sixty/Sixty-Five was available with extra heavy-duty options to meet a variety of working situations. This tractor is configured with a factory heavy-duty radiator guard and curved bumper, along with a front-mounted tow hook. This setup was most likely for a logging or forestry application. It's quite rare today to find one of these vintage diesel tractors with these options. *Courtesy Caterpillar, Inc. Corporate Archives*

DIESEL SIXTY-FIVE
A special "cold-weather" package was also offered for the Diesel Sixty/Sixty-Five that included a fully enclosed heated cab, a rear mounted fuel tank, and a completely shrouded engine compartment. This option group gave the tractor a very complete and modern look for its day. *courtesy of Caterpillar, Inc. Corporate Archives*

Even though Caterpillar was convinced it had the product everyone wanted, the sales staff did not sit back and let the machine sell itself. Instead, the company launched an aggressive sales pitch in all corners of the United States and foreign countries, too. Dealers were urged to ensure that the first diesel tractors in any area went to influential owners. They were also recommended to sell the new diesel tractors to customers close to their home base so the servicemen could make frequent calls and jump on any minor problems that might arise. One-day dealer courses were set up all over the country, and special "diesel shows" were presented to tens of thousands of prospective customers to demonstrate the diesel's advantages.

From the outset, Caterpillar Tractor Company intended to maximize the use of its diesel engine in as many applications as possible. Running parallel with tractor development, Caterpillar put together a marketing team to exploit its new, efficient engine in many different markets. Already well established in the stationary gasoline engine business, the company naturally pursued a similar market for its diesel product. The economies of diesel power and lower fuel cost were an even greater advantage to the stationary engine customer, with his higher annual operating hours. Tractor owners typically operated a tractor for about 2,000 hours per year, whereas a stationary engine generating electricity for

a small industrial plant, pumping water in an irrigation project, or running an air compressor, could easily rack up 6,000 or 7,000 hours per year. Given that the annual depreciation cost is fixed, simple economics proved to owners that more could be saved from lower fuel cost in a higher-hour unit, because fuel is the largest single expense in those units.

Caterpillar sold its first non-tractor diesel engine to crane and excavator maker Thew Shovel Company of Lorain, Ohio. After it was successfully installed and operated in one of their 1-1/2-yard Lorain 75B models, it didn't take long for manufacturers of compressors, gravel plants, drill rigs, and locomotives, as well as other excavator builders, to recognize the diesel's advantages. From nine non-tractor customers in 1932, the number increased to 17 the following year. Customers doubled in 1934 and rose to over 100 by 1938. The diesel engine rapidly became one of Caterpillar's main products. As early as 1933, Caterpillar produced more diesel horsepower than the rest of the nation's manufacturers had, combined, during the preceding year. By 1937, Caterpillar's diesel production totaled more than 660,000 horsepower, and still accounted for one-third of the U.S. total, even though all major manufacturers were entering this market. Caterpillar was a key figure in the development of the modern diesel engine, not only in tractors but in all applications.

CHAPTER FIVE

GAS AND DIESEL SHARE THE LIMELIGHT

The first Caterpillar Diesel tractor was launched in 1931, and by the end of the decade, diesel had almost eclipsed gasoline power in crawler tractors. Only the small R2, R4, and R5 gas models remained in Caterpillar's product line, and even those were discontinued during World War II. This transition to diesel power over such a comparatively short period was attributable in a large part to Caterpillar's aggressive marketing strategy throughout the 1930s. Starting in the midst of the worst depression in industrial history, Caterpillar managed to overcome diesel fuel manufacturing and distribution problems, and convert nearly all of its customers to the diesel tractor, a machine promising lower-cost, high-efficiency operations. But the gasoline tractors did not go out quietly.

In fact, gasoline tractors continued to sell very well throughout the 1930s, taking the Great Depression into account. Strong support persisted for gas-powered equipment despite the generally depressed market. Recognizing this demand, Caterpillar launched progressively larger gas tractors during this period. With the diesel engine slowly

Diesel Seventy-Five
The Diesel Seventy was replaced in mid-1933 with the Caterpillar Seventy-Five (S.N. prefix 2E). The Diesel Seventy-Five was powered by the improved Cat D11000, six-cylinder, 51/4x8-inch bore and stroke, diesel engine. This tractor shared most of its undercarriage with the Diesel Seventy, including the 78-inch track gauge. This Diesel Seventy-Five is a 1934 model, serial number 2E452.
Tyler Family. *ECO*

DIESEL THIRTY-FIVE
Caterpillar introduced its Diesel Thirty-Five (S.N. prefix 6E) in 1933. It was powered by a Cat D6100, three-cylinder 5-1/4x8-inch bore-and-stroke diesel engine. Pictured is an ultra-rare, 1934 tailseat "orchard" Diesel Thirty-Five (S.N. 6E820). *ECO*

DIESEL THIRTY-FIVE
The Diesel Thirty-Five was originally released in 1933 in 53-inch narrow-gauge and 74-inch wide-gauge configurations. Starting with serial No. 6E230 in that same year, the 53-inch offering was changed to 56 inches. The Diesel Thirty-Five was produced through 1934, with approximately 1,999 units built. Only a very small number of these were of the tailseat variety. *ECO*

gaining popularity, the company offered most new models in the early 1930s with either gasoline or diesel power.

The Fifty (5A-series) gasoline-powered tractor was released in 1931. This was powered by a Caterpillar 7500G, four-cylinder 5-1/2x6-1/2-inch bore-and-stroke gasoline engine rated at 50-drawbar horsepower and 55-belt horsepower at 850 rpm. The early Fifty tractors were identified with the word FIFTY cast into the sides of the radiator, and the fuel tank was located in front of the driver. But by 1933 the radiator name casting was removed from the sides and placed on top of the radiator front, and the fuel tank was incorporated into the seat back. At the same time, the firewall and instrument panel were redesigned, and engine power was increased to 52.65-drawbar horsepower and 60.13-belt horsepower.

THIRTY-FIVE

The gasoline-powered Caterpillar Thirty-Five (S.N. prefix 5C) was first introduced in 1932. Engine of choice was the Cat 6000G, four-cylinder 4-7/8x6-1/2-inch bore-and-stroke motor. Initially, 53-inch narrow-gauge and 74-inch wide-gauge track layouts were offered. In 1934, starting with serial No. 5C1525, the narrow-gauge was upped to 56 inches. When production ended in early 1935 (eleven tractors built in 1935 to use up existing engine surplus), some 1,730 tractors had been produced. This vintage 1932 Thirty-Five (S.N. 5C515) is a narrow-gauge model. *ECO*

Also in 1933, Caterpillar introduced the Fifty's diesel counterpart, the Diesel Fifty (1E-series). This came equipped with the Caterpillar D7700, four-cylinder 5-1/4x8-inch bore-and-stroke engine producing 56.03-drawbar horsepower and 65.6-belt horsepower at 850 rpm. Both Fifty versions were equipped with a four-speed transmission giving speeds from 1.6 to 4.7 miles per hour, and both were offered with either standard 60-inch or wide-gauge 74-inch track widths. The wide-gauge option gained its greatest advantage on steep hillsides or over soft ground, and the wider track position matched the gauge of standard hauling wagons and allowed the tractor to straddle wide windrows. The Fifty weighed 18,080 pounds in its standard form, and the Diesel Fifty weighed 20,250 pounds.

FORTY

The Caterpillar Forty (S.N. prefix 5G) was introduced in late 1934 as the replacement for the Thirty-Five. The Forty was powered by a Cat 6500G, four-cylinder 5-1/8x6-1/2-inch bore-and-stroke gasoline engine. Track gauge offerings were 56 and 74 inches. Production would end in 1936 with only 584 tractors built. This 1935 vintage Forty (S.N. 5G130 SP) is a much-sought-after wide-gauge configuration. *ECO*

DIESEL FORTY
The Caterpillar Diesel Forty (S.N. prefix 3G) was introduced in late 1934 at the same time as the gasoline-powered Forty, and was available in the same track gauge widths as that model. The Diesel Forty was powered by the same three-cylinder Cat D6100 diesel engine formerly in the Diesel Thirty-Five, with a few extra ponies dialed in. Production ended in 1936 with 1,971 tractors. *Courtesy Caterpillar, Inc. Corporate Archives*

The Diesel Fifty ended its production run in 1936, and the gas-powered Fifty held on for one more year. Even though the production run for the Fifty was a year longer than its diesel brother, its sales accounted for 1,707 units, some 12 percent less than the 2,065 diesel units shipped to customers. These sales figures were typical of other tractor models of the era that were offered with both types of power. In most cases the diesel version outsold the gas counterpart as diesel gained ground in most crawler tractor applications.

With the tractor improvements on the Fifty series tractors, and the newly adopted Hi-Way Yellow paint,

FIFTY
In late 1931, Caterpillar introduced its Fifty (S.N. prefix 5A) gasoline-powered tractor. The original Fifty was powered by a Cat 7500G, four-cylinder 5-1/2x6-1/2-inch bore-and-stroke gas motor. Track gauge offerings were 60 and 74 inches. The early Fifty had its fuel tank mounted in front of the operator, and also had the word "FIFTY" cast on the radiator sides. *Courtesy Caterpillar, Inc. Corporate Archives*

Caterpillar hoped to pull the stagnant tractor market out of the doldrums. But it would still be a few years before the company was able to report extensive sales on any of its new models. Farmers and contractors were still reeling from the Great Depression and did not yet have money to spend on new equipment. In the meantime, Caterpillar remained determined to claim the lion's share of what little tractor market there was, and in keeping with its aggressive development policy, brought out more new models to replace existing ones.

Caterpillar launched the Thirty-Five (5C-series) in 1932, and the Diesel Thirty-Five (6E-series) the following year. The Thirty-Five replaced the former Thirty (PS-series) and carried a Caterpillar 6000G, four-cylinder 4-7/8x6-1/2-inch bore-and-stroke gasoline engine rated at 37-drawbar horsepower and 41-belt-horsepower at 850 rpm. The Diesel Thirty-Five was fitted with the D6100, three-cylinder 5-1/4x8-inch bore-and-stroke engine rated at 38.65-drawbar horsepower and 46.08-belt-horsepower. Both gasoline and diesel versions were equipped with a four-speed transmission that delivered speeds from 1.7 to 4.6 miles per hour. Shipping weights were 12,480 pounds and 13,900 pounds, respectively. The Thirty-Five series tractors were originally sold with a 53-inch track gauge, but this was increased to a standard 56-inch gauge some time in 1934. A 74-inch wide-gauge version was available throughout the model run. To maximize the advantages of the wide-gauge option, and recommended for work on steep hillsides or soft ground, the standard 16-inch track shoes could be replaced with 18-inch or 20-inch shoes.

The Thirty-Five series tractors were similar to the Fifty series with sheet-metal work covering the engine, and substantial sheeting around the operator's seat area. One exception was the "orchard special," on which the operator sat on a cantilevered sprung seat over the rear of the tractor. Many of the models from the early to mid-1930s sold in relatively low numbers. Total sales for the Thirty-Five 5C tractor amounted to 1,730 units, while the diesel 6E model racked up 1,999 sales.

The Thirty-Five had a very short production life, with both gasoline and diesel versions replaced by the Forty (5G-series) and Diesel Forty (3G-series) in 1934. The Forty was powered by a 6500G, four-cylinder 5-1/8x6-1/2-inch bore-and-stroke gasoline engine with 42-drawbar horsepower and 48-belt horsepower. The Diesel Forty carried the same D6100, three-cylinder diesel engine as its predecessor, but was rated a little higher at 44-drawbar horsepower and 49-belt horsepower. Both the Forty and Diesel Forty were built with a 56-inch track gauge in their standard form, and like the former Thirty Five models, wide-gauge variations were also offered with track centers spaced 74 inches apart. The standard 16-inch track shoes could be exchanged for shoes 18 inches, 20 inches, or 24 inches wide. An even wider 30-inch angle track shoe was also available for extremely soft conditions. The Thirty-Five and Forty series tractors looked similar in both diesel and gasoline versions when

viewed side-by-side, with only a few changes made to the undercarriage design to aid manufacture. The Forty and Diesel Forty weighed 13,310 pounds and 14,700 pounds, respectively. The gas-powered 5G sold only 584 units, while sales of the diesel 3G ran to 1,971 units.

In 1932, Caterpillar presented the Sixty-Five (2D-series) as the official replacement for the gas Sixty. The company most likely had high hopes for this model as it replaced the tractor that had been so successful. But like others released during this economically depressed era,

sales proved disappointing to Caterpillar management. The low sales must have been even more disappointing to the designers of this radical-looking tractor. It looked quite different from anything Caterpillar had produced before. With ample sheet metal, its rounded top hood and curved radiator front with the words SIXTY FIVE cast on both sides gave this tractor a decidedly modern look, even for today. Under the hood, a Caterpillar 9000G, four-cylinder 7x8-1/2-inch bore-and-stroke gasoline engine provided the power. It was rated at

DIESEL FIFTY
Caterpillar introduced the gas Fifty's counterpart, the Diesel Fifty (S.N. prefix 1E), in 1933. The Diesel Fifty was powered by a Cat D7700, four-cylinder 5-1/4x8-inch bore-and-stroke diesel engine. Track gauges were the same as the gasoline-powered Fifty. Production ended in early 1936 with 2,065 tractors manufactured. Shown is a 1934 narrow-gauge Diesel Fifty (1E1159). Owner: George E. Logue. *ECO*

Those who purchased this well-designed tractor were rewarded with a solid producer that exceeded expectations. When the Sixty-Five ended its short production run in 1933, only 521 units had been sold.

In 1933, Caterpillar introduced the next new tractors—the Seventy (8D-series) and Diesel Seventy (3E-series). The Seventy was the ultimate in big gas tractors, and turned out to be the most powerful ever produced by Caterpillar. Its engine was the Caterpillar 9500G, with four cylinders of 7x8-1/2-inch bore and stroke. Initially advertised as 76-drawbar horsepower and 87-belt horsepower tractor, its ratings were increased to 77.07 and 89.43 soon after its introduction. The Diesel Seventy carried the same D9900, four-cylinder diesel found in the previous Diesel Sixty/Sixty Five, but it was up-rated to 76-drawbar horsepower and 87-belt horsepower. Both Seventy tractors bore the same sheet-metal design, except for different allowances in the hood for air cleaner and exhaust pipe openings. Both were designed

SIXTY-FIVE
Introduced in 1932, the gasoline-powered Caterpillar Sixty-Five was the only tractor model series to wear this type of bodywork. With its tall radiator housing and rounded hood, it is considered by many to be the most visually striking of all Caterpillar Tractor Company designs. But others felt it sort of resembled a mechanical "pachyderm." Pictured is a vintage 1932 Sixty-Five (S.N. 2D453) equipped with the optional logging front bumper. *ECO*

68-drawbar horsepower and 79-belt horsepower. The frame and undercarriage were based on the recently introduced Diesel Sixty, and not carried forward from the former gas Sixty tractor. However, the frame rails were shortened to accommodate the more compact gasoline engine. The track gauge was 72 inches, and its shipping weight was listed as just over 23,000 pounds. The Sixty Five's radical appearance may have worked against it. Some called it ugly, others loved its sleek lines, but in the end it was certainly a creation ahead of its time.

Sixty-Five
The production life of the Caterpillar Sixty-five was brief. Commenced in 1932, production would end in mid-1933, after only 521 tractors were built. The short run of this unique Caterpillar model can be blamed on customers' change in tastes from big gasoline to big diesel powered tractors. The Sixty-Five's outdated undercarriage and questionable aesthetics did not help matters any. *ECO*

SEVENTY
The Caterpillar gas Sixty-Five was essentially replaced in 1933 by the Seventy (S.N. prefix 8D) model line. The Seventy was a totally new design that shared nothing with the Sixty-Five. It was powered by a Cat 9500G, four-cylinder, 7x8-1/2-inch bore-and-stroke gasoline engine. It was only offered in a 78-inch track gauge. But in the end, only 266 tractors were produced before the plug was pulled on the model in early 1937. This rare Seventy (S.N. 8D158) is a 1934 model equipped with the optional heavy-duty radiator guard. Owner: Don Dougherty. *ECO*

DIESEL SEVENTY
Rarest of the early large diesel Caterpillar tractors is the Diesel Seventy (S.N. prefix 3E). Produced only in 1933, with just 51 machines assembled, it was rare even when new. The Diesel Seventy was powered by the same engine found in the earlier Diesel Sixty/Sixty-Five, the D9900. The track gauge was 78 inches. But problems with the D9900 in this model caused many of the engines to be pulled by the dealers and replaced with the improved D11000 diesel. There are no restored examples of this tractor known to exist. *ECO Collection*

with a 78-inch track gauge, and the tractors weighed 31,070 and 30,800 pounds, respectively.

Sales expectations for the Seventy series were high. The new tractors were designed with the customer in mind and with all the experience the largest tractor-maker could muster. But again, the depressed market overcame the enthusiasm, and sales were terribly disappointing. The Diesel Seventy was withdrawn from the market the same year it was introduced, after achieving sales of only 51 units. The gas-powered Seventy fared a little better, but total sales of only 266 units over its four-year production run up to 1937 sent a strong message to Caterpillar management. Basically, Caterpillar would no longer pursue gasoline power in large crawler tractors. It would continue to make gasoline versions of its existing small models for as long as the market held up.

Throughout the Depression years of the 1930s, Caterpillar never rested on its laurels, or sat back to see how the market would develop. The company aggressively sought out its own markets, rectified design problems, and introduced new models as quickly as it phased out old ones, or more so. Some models had disappointingly short production runs, but this did nothing more than to spur Caterpillar on to new innovations. When the Diesel Seventy, with the old D9900 engine, failed to garner sales, it was immediately

replaced in 1933 with the Diesel Seventy-Five tractor, sporting a new engine. It was Caterpillar's largest tractor to date, carrying the new D11000 six-cylinder diesel, with 5-1/4x8-inch bore and stroke, 83.23-drawbar horsepower, and 98.01-belt horsepower. The new tractor ran on basically the same undercarriage and track gauge as the Seventy series, but the frame was redesigned to accommodate the six-cylinder diesel.

Even this "super" tractor did not bring the house down in sales. Approximately 1,078 units were shipped to customers over its production run up to 1935. These numbers may appear disappointing, but all was not lost. The comparatively low sales of the Diesel Seventy-Five disguised the fact that a new generation of large diesel tractors was born. The experience gained from these early diesel tractors would put Caterpillar on a firm footing, not only during World War II, but for decades to come. These large tractors were ideal for pushing with bulldozer blades, ripping, or pulling scrapers, and they soon found themselves at home on some of the largest earthmoving projects of the era. Now, for the first time, Caterpillar turned its focus from agriculture to the emerging earthmoving industry.

The advent of the diesel engine allowed Caterpillar to broaden its markets into the heavy construction and surface mining fields, but the company never forgot its

farming roots and continued to serve that market with crawler tractors. We shall see in chapter 7 that during the 1980s and 1990s Caterpillar introduced many new farming products including a line of rubber-tracked tractors. Also in the 1990s, the company started once more to market combines, a product with a company heritage going back to Caterpillar's very roots—built long before the crawler tractor by Caterpillar's founders, Holt and Best.

TRACTOR ATTACHMENTS

The success of the crawler tractor spawned a whole new industry of tractor attachment makers. Once the crawler tractor's reliability had been perfected around the time of Caterpillar Tractor Company's formation in 1925, entrepreneurs began to realize that such mobile power offered all kinds of opportunities to actuate mechanical equipment in industries other than farming. Contrivances for pushing, pulling, lifting, compacting, hauling, ripping,

SIXTY-FIVE

The Caterpillar Sixty-Five was powered by a Cat 9000G, four-cylinder 7x8-1/2-inch bore-and-stroke gasoline engine. The undercarriage of the tractor was based on the design of the Diesel Sixty/Sixty-Five, and not on the gas Sixty. Only one track gauge of 72 inches was offered. This image of a Sixty-Five (S.N. 2D358) is a 1932 vintage tractor equipped with the optional heavy-duty crankcase guard and front tow hook. Owner: Tyler family. *ECO*

suffered major flooding, Holt's people bolted a plank onto the front frame of one of their big steam wheel tractors to clear debris from the streets, but neither Holt nor Best expressed any interest in making such attachments. They were tractor builders pure and simple.

The tractor builders' reluctance to make auxiliary equipment for their own tractors opened the door for many small companies in the 1920s to enter the new business. With attachment builders appearing almost by the month, some control had to be taken. There were well-designed, robust attachments, but there were also ill-designed items that fell apart at the first sign of tough work. Such failures might give the Caterpillar tractor a poor reputation. So Caterpillar undertook to put each piece of auxiliary equipment through an approval process with the objective of allowing only officially approved attachments to work with its tractors. A routine was thus established in the 1920s, whereby any manufacturer wanting to make an attachment for a Caterpillar tractor had to submit designs and obtain approval from Caterpillar engineers. Once approved, the attachment maker's products would be marketed through the network of Caterpillar dealers.

By the early 1930s, over 80 auxiliary products were approved for use with Caterpillar tractors, including bulldozer blades made by 11 different firms, and 20 brands of scrapers. The table in this chapter shows Caterpillar-approved companies and products as listed for the year 1932. However, starting in the mid-1930s, the list of auxiliary manufacturers began to shorten. Some went out of business, but the major attachment manufacturers started to align themselves with certain brands of tractors, designing equipment suitable for one particular make. This was particularly true in the case of scraper and bulldozer blade manufacturers, who eventually entered into exclusive arrangements with the tractor builders. Under these arrangements, manufacturers supplied tractors exclusively fitted with a certain brand of auxiliary equipment.

After World War II, the major tractor makers finally started to build attachments designed for their own tractors (see Chapter 6). But this did not put the attachment builders out of business. Such was the demand for equipment that ample room still existed for the specialist auxiliary equipment builders, provided they made a reliable and innovative

cutting, drilling, and log skidding rapidly came on the scene from a multitude of manufacturers. This auxiliary equipment was driven from the tractor's PTO, or hung on the front, back, side, or mounted on top of the tractor. The tractor builders themselves had made it clear that they were not interested in taking up valuable shop space for fabricating dozer blades, scrapers, and the like, or using costly engineer's time to design working attachments. As far back as 1908, when the center of Stockton

product. The ideas for many attachments often came from the customer or tractor operator. An example occurred in 1945 when a contractor requested a Florida company to make a special land-clearing rake. It was so successful that other customers requested the company make similar land-clearing devices. The result was the Florida Land Clearing Equipment Company (Fleco), whose land-clearing rakes, stump cutters, and tree dozers became popular products sold through Caterpillar dealers.

Many other names became famous because of their association with Caterpillar Tractor Company. The Trackson Company produced dump wagons mounted on crawler wheels of its own design. In 1936 it started to fit side booms on Caterpillar tractors, followed by a cable-operated front-end loader the following year. Its loaders and side-boom pipelayers worked so well that Caterpillar eventually purchased Trackson in 1951 (see Chapter 6). The Hyster Company, famous for forklift trucks, produced winches, logging arches, and an excavator called the Hystaway that mounted on the back of a tractor. With a separate seat, the excavator was fully convertible to crane, dragline, clamshell, shovel, and hoe. The Athey Products Corporation built earth wagons for hauling behind Caterpillar tractors, and applied its Forged Track crawler mounting to trailers hauled by crawler tractors. Later, Athey side-dumping, bottom-dumping, and rear-dumping wagons became a natural match for Caterpillar's high-speed wheeled tractors in the 1950s. Athey also designed a cable-operated loader called the "MobiLoader" for mounting on crawler tractors. This device could dig in front, then hoist its load up and over, and dump in the rear without turning the tractor. Among the other famous names synonymous with Caterpillar tractors are the American Tractor Equipment Company (Ateco) and Kelly Ripper, both of whom build rippers. Balderson made a name for itself with its super-sized dozer blades for pushing light materials like coal or wood chips. Caterpillar purchased a majority interest in Balderson in 1990. Then there was a whole host of pull-type scraper builders, some of whom are still supplying scrapers for Caterpillar tractors today.

Auxiliary equipment manufacturers typically build their products on a scale smaller than would be feasible at Caterpillar. But they are well equipped to provide specialized knowledge and after-sales support that meet Caterpillar's standards. Their working arrangement with Caterpillar provides them with a ready-made sales organization through Cat's dealer network, and in turn, Caterpillar is able to expand the application of its tractors, and hence increase sales.

CATERPILLAR-APPROVED AUXILIARY EQUIPMENT BUILDERS FOR 1932

COMPANY NAME	PRODUCTS
Allsteel Products Mfg. Co.	Pipelayers, winches, pumps, Cardwell side-boom backfiller
American Hoist & Derrick Co.	American-deVou derrick crane—swings 180 degrees
American Steam Pump Co.	PTO-driven pumps
American Tractor Equipment Co.	Bulldozer blades, rollers, rippers, pull-scrapers
Ann Arbor Machine Co.	Rollers
Anthony Company, Inc.	Cable-operated front end loader
Paul Arbon & Co.	Winches
Athey Truss Wheel Co.	Winches, crawler trailers, crawler wagons
Atlas Scraper Co.	Drag scrapers
Baker Manufacturing Co.	Bulldozer blades, disks, rippers, drag scrapers, Baker-Maney scrapers
Otto Biefeld Co.	Snow plows
Blair Manufacturing Co.	Cable-operated front-end loader
Blaw-Knox Co.	Bulldozer blades, rollers, rippers, scrapers
Bodinson Mfg. Co., Inc.	Rollers, rippers, scrapers
Braden Steel Winch Co.	Winches
Wm. Bros Boiler & Mfg. Co.	Bulldozer blades
Bucyrus-Erie Co.	Loadmaster 360-degree cranes
The Buda Company	Buda-Hubron earth drill
Commercial Shearing Co.	Scrapers
Conco Crane & Engineering Wks.	Bottom dump wagons
Contractors Machinery Corp.	Rippers, Trojan drag scrapers

Davey Compressor Co.	Air compressors
Davis Manufacturing Co.	Bulldozer blades, scrapers
Day Pulverizer Co., Inc.	Portable crushers
Detroit Harvester Co.	Brooms
Dorsey Brothers	Stump pullers
Easton Car & Const. Co.	Wagons
Electric Wheel Company	Wheel trailers, crawler trailers, wagons
Euclid Road Machinery Co.	Bulldozer blades, rollers, scrapers, crawler wagons
Farm Tools, Inc.	Drag scrapers
Alex Feigelson	Trailers
Garland Wagon Co.	Trailers, skidders
Gifford-Wood Co.	Ice levelers
Havana Metal Wheel Co.	Trailers
Hester Plow Co.	Plows
Highway Trailer Co.	Earth borers, winches, scrapers, trailers
Hopper Machine Works, Inc.	Winches
Hughes-Keenan Co.	Roustabout 360-degree cranes
Isaacson Iron Works	Bulldozer blades, rippers
Jumbo Scraper Co.	Scrapers
Killefer Mfg. Corp. Ltd.	Disks, plows, rippers, scrapers
The Knight Company	Pull rippers
Lakewood Engineering Co.	Pull rippers
LaPlant-Choate Mfg. Co., Inc.	Bulldozer blades, Bull-scoop, rollers, rippers, scrapers, crawler wagons, wheel wagons, and trailers
Lenhart Wagon Co.	Wagons
R.G. LeTourneau, Inc.	Bulldozer blades, scrapers, winches, rollers, side booms, rippers, wagons
Lindsey Wagon Co.	Trailers, skidders
Luther Mfg. Co., Inc.	Winches
Maine Steel Products Co.	Snow plows
Martin Wagon Co.	Trailers
Master Equipment Co.	Bulldozer blades, drag scrapers, pipelayers
Miami Trailer-Scraper Co.	Bulldozer blades, scrapers, front-end loader, wagons, trailers
Niess & Co., Inc.	Bulldozer blades
Oliver Farm Equipment Co.	Plows
Pacific Car & Foundry Co.	Logging arches and winches under brand name CARCO
Pacific Gear & Tool Works	Winches
Pioneer Gravel Equipment Co.	Double drum winches
Ransomes Sims & Jefferies Ltd.	Drag scrapers
Rotary Snow Plow Co.	Rotary snow plows
Schramm, Inc.	Air compressors, portable welders
Sidney Steel Scraper Co.	Drag scrapers
Silent Hoist Winch & Crane Co.	Winches
Slusser-McLean Scraper Co.	Drag scrapers
Spears-Wells Machinery Co.	Pull-type pavement profilers
A. Streich & Bros. Co.	Wagons, trailers, skidders
Towner Mfg. Co.	Scrapers, rippers, disks
Trackson Co.	Crawler wagons
Trail-It Co.	Wagons
Utility Supply Co.	Cable-laying plows, cable reelers
Western Enterprise Engine Co.	Winches
Willamette-Ersted Co.	Logging arches, winches, front booms, scrapers (Products designed by HYSTER)
W-K-M Company	Side booms

CHAPTER SIX

THE ADVENT OF CONSTRUCTION EQUIPMENT

Several factors contributed to Caterpillar Tractor Company's expansion into the heavy construction equipment business in the mid-1930s. The world was just getting back on its feet after the Depression, and money started trickling back into contractors' pockets. The economy was further spurred on by massive U.S. government projects on which Caterpillar could foresee a market for its products. Contractors needed heavy equipment to move millions of cubic yards of earth, and with the introduction of the new diesel tractors, Caterpillar had the technology to fill this need, and also move forward with equipment even larger than it presently offered.

Caterpillar had already aligned itself with the construction and road-building equipment industry when it purchased the Russell Grader Manufacturing Company in 1928. Founded in 1903 by Richard Russell and C.K. Stockland, in Stephen, Minnesota, the company moved to Minneapolis shortly afterwards. Early products included a horse-drawn elevating grader, plows, and various pull-type graders and scrapers. By 1908 the company introduced a grader specifically designed to be pulled by a tractor. Russell launched larger pull-type graders over the years leading up to the Caterpillar takeover. More significant was the company's self-propelled grader, the prototype of which was

RD8 AND DIESEL SEVENTY-FIVE
The Caterpillar RD8 replaced the Diesel Seventy-Five in 1935 as top tractor in the company's product line. Pictured is a 1936 RD8 (S.N. 1H698) parked next to a 1934 Diesel Seventy-Five (S.N. 2E452). Owner: Tyler family. *ECO*

RD8

The Caterpillar RD8 was originally introduced in 1935 equipped with the D11000 engine (S.N. prefix 5E8001). After only 33 tractors, it was replaced the same year with the 1H-series RD8, featuring the newly designed Cat D13000, six-cylinder 5-3/4x8-inch bore-and-stroke diesel engine. Track gauge was 78 inches. The 1H-series RD8 became the 1H-series D8 in late 1937. Production would end on the 1H-series RD8/D8 in 1941, with a total of 9,999 tractors coming off the assembly line. This RD8 is a vintage 1935 model, serial No. 1H49. Owner: George E. Logue. *ECO*

D8

The Caterpillar crawler tractor played a key roll in Allied operations in the European and Pacific campaigns during World War II. This D8 (S.N. prefix 8R) is a U.S. Army issued tractor awaiting shipping from Peoria, equipped with a LeTourneau CK8 Angledozer blade. The 8R-series was in production from 1941 to 1945, with 9,999 machines produced. *ECO Collection*

built in 1919. It appeared on the market in 1920 as the Motor Hi-Way Patrol No. 1, and was built around an Allis-Chalmers two-wheel tractor. This machine is acknowledged as the industry's first self-propelled grader, and at the time it attracted much attention. Russell worked with other manufacturers, designing grader attachments for Fordson, McCormick-Deering, Cletrac, and Caterpillar tractors. The latter two companies provided crawler tractors that were mounted behind Russell's grader attachment. The Motor Patrol No. 4 from late 1926 was based on a Caterpillar 2-Ton tractor, and the Motor Patrol No. 6, introduced in 1928, was based on a Caterpillar Twenty tractor.

With a close collaboration already established, Caterpillar favored the Russell company when it was ready to expand into the road-building market. The Russell takeover put Caterpillar in the grader business, and the company quickly set about realigning the former Russell product lines to fit its own. Caterpillar sold off any products and designs that were not directly associated with its

D8
This Caterpillar D8 (S.N. prefix 2U) from September 1946 is equipped with a Cat No. 8S Bulldozer straight blade and early production No. 46 Hydraulic Control. This was the first commercial hydraulic blade control offered by the company. The 2U-series was in production from late 1945 to 1953, with a whopping 23,537 tractors manufactured, all with the D13000 diesel powerplant. *ECO Collection*

own equipment. The company retained the pull-type, elevating, and self-propelled graders lines, and from 1930, started to revise the designs to bring them into line with Caterpillar's standards. By the end of the 1930s, it dropped the pull-type grader line. The elevating graders were manufactured until 1942. The self-propelled grader, however, was quite a different story. Caterpillar continued to make extensive technological changes over the years, and today, motor graders are one of the company's most important product lines.

Another important event influenced Caterpillar's decision to enter the construction equipment market: earthmoving equipment maker, R.G. LeTourneau, opened a new plant in the company's hometown of Peoria, Illinois. Starting business as an earthmoving contractor in Stockton, California, the now legendary R.G. LeTourneau began building his own equipment for use on his contracts when suppliers could not provide exactly what he wanted.

Although LeTourneau experimented with many types of earthmoving equipment, including a self-propelled electrically operated scraper as early as 1923, his most notable achievement was a very effective pull-type scraper that could be towed behind any make of crawler tractor. He first modified a Schmeiser pull-type scraper in 1920, and by 1922, he had built a scraper of welded construction called the "Gondola." R.G. LeTourneau, Inc. was incorporated in Stockton in 1929, and the company gained fame by completing the access road contract for the famous Hoover Dam. Soon afterward R.G. LeTourneau withdrew from contracting to concentrate on equipment manufacture. In 1932, after building and using many different types of scrapers, LeTourneau designed a four-wheel pull-type scraper he called a "Carryall," the first to be mounted on rubber tires. The patented design was eventually made in many different models and capacities to match all sizes of crawler tractors on the market.

D8

The Caterpillar D8 model line was a contractor's dream come true. Its power, size, and reliability were unmatched in the marketplace. This D8 tractor is a 1954 model, serial No. 13A2485 SP, with a No. 80 scraper in tow. The 13A-series was first released in 1953, and ended production in 1955 with 3,703 tractors built. Owner: Ed Akin. *ECO*

To operate his scrapers, LeTourneau invented a reliable power control unit (PCU) in 1928 that mounted on a crawler tractor. Driven from the tractor's PTO, the PCU was essentially a double drum winch controlled by levers operating individual clutches and brakes. It could control the scraper bowl lift, apron lift, and ejector through two cables. The PCU could not only operate a pull-type scraper, but also dozer blades, rippers, and other attachments. The PCU was regarded as the greatest innovation to transform the crawler tractor into an earthmover. With this well-designed tractor equipment, R.G. LeTourneau had built a solid reputation as a supplier to all the major tractor manufacturers of the day, including Cletrac, Allis-Chalmers, International Harvester, and Caterpillar.

Several other pull-type scraper and bulldozer blade manufacturers also appeared in the 1930s. At that time, the major tractor builders had no desire to take up valuable shop space to manufacture bulky fabrications such as scrapers and dozer blades. They preferred to leave that up

D8

This pilot D8 tractor from August 1954 is equipped with the first prototype turbocharged engine ever installed in the model line. But it would not be until 1958 that the turbocharged engine would become a production reality with the release of the direct drive 36A-series D8H, equipped with the D342 diesel engine. *ECO Collection*

MRD7
The Caterpillar RD7 was an excellent agricultural tractor for big field jobs, but was an equally magnificent dozing machine. This late model RD7 is equipped with a LeTourneau E7 Bulldozer blade with a rear-mounted cable power control unit. Two track gauges of 60 and 74 inches were offered. At the end of 1937, the 9G-series RD7 became the 9G-series D7. Production would last until 1940, with a total of 7,254 tractors built.
ECO Collection

to specialist attachment suppliers who sold their products through the tractor dealers. Initially customers could choose which make of blade or other attachment would be attached to their new tractor. As time went on, the major attachment manufacturers aligned themselves with certain tractor manufacturers so that eventually, exclusive arrangements were made. This was particularly true in the case of scrapers and bulldozer blades, where a certain brand would be supplied exclusively for a certain brand of tractor.

One prime example of a tractor-attachment alliance was the agreement reached in 1934 between Caterpillar Tractor Company and R.G. LeTourneau, Inc. It provided for the network of Caterpillar dealers across the United States to market the full line of LeTourneau earthmoving equipment. This agreement, however, did not limit the Caterpillar deal-

ers from carrying other brands of allied tractor equipment, which of course could be operated on Caterpillar tractors.

To help in the production and delivery of equipment, LeTourneau expanded east in 1935, and built a large new factory just down the street and across the Illinois River from Caterpillar's own East Peoria plant. LeTourneau chose this site to nurture the newly established collaboration between the two companies. New tractors could now be sent over to LeTourneau with negligible shipping cost, to be fitted with power control units, bulldozer blades, or other accessories before being shipped out to the dealers by truck, rail, or barge.

Caterpillar's largest diesel tractor, the Diesel Seventy-Five, was not exactly a resounding success in terms of sales, but was a milestone and forerunner of a very long and suc-

cessful line of large diesel tractors. It was replaced in 1935 by the RD8. This model designation was in line with the new numbering system adopted by Caterpillar a year earlier with the introduction of the R2, R3, and R5. The RD8 (5E8001) was basically the same design, and carried the same engine, as the Diesel Seventy-Five but had a slightly higher horsepower rating. Only 33 of the first-series RD8s found their way to customers, but the RD8 (1H-series) that came out later the same year really put Caterpillar's diesel

tractors on the map. Sporting the new D13000 six-cylinder diesel under the hood, it was rated at 95-drawbar horsepower and 110-belt horsepower with a 5-3/4x8-inch bore and stroke. Its track gauge measured 78 inches. In late 1937 the 1H-series RD8 was renamed the D8 to avoid confusion with the R-series gasoline models, but the tractor remained the same. Approximately 9,999 1H tractors were produced until 1941, by which time its power had increased to 113-drawbar horsepower and 132-belt horsepower.

The Caterpillar RD7 was first introduced in 1935 as the replacement for the Diesel Fifty. The first series of RD7 tractors (S.N. prefix 5E7501) were based on Diesel Fifty mechanicals, including the drivetrain, with only 25 produced. In that same year, a far more improved RD7 (S.N. prefix 9G) was introduced, equipped with a Cat D8800, four-cylinder 5-3/4x8-inch bore-and-stroke diesel engine. Pictured is a 1936 vintage, narrow-gauge RD7 (S.N. 9G1972 SP). Owner: Tyler family. *ECO*

D7

Like the D8, the Caterpillar D7 played an important roll for the Allied troops during World War II from opening up beach heads to building air strips. This 1945 vintage D7 is an authentic military issue tractor, carrying serial No. 3T1651 SP. The 3T-series was manufactured from 1944 to 1955, with 28,058 tractors built, all with a 74-inch track gauge. Owner: Tyler family. *ECO*

In 1941, Caterpillar launched an upgraded model of the D8 with serial number prefix 8R. It received some mechanical design refinements, but its outward appearance was very similar to its predecessor, and it carried the same D13000 engine. The 8R-series D8 was produced in the same quantity as the 1H, with 9,999 built through 1945. This was the tractor, along with the D7 described later, that spearheaded the war effort for the United States and its allies during World War II. Equipped with a

LeTourneau bulldozer blade or Carryall scraper, the tractor was almost unstoppable. In fact, the government required almost all of the equipment Caterpillar and LeTourneau could produce, and with the companies' plants located in close proximity in Peoria, productivity from this winning team soared, and tractors were shipped by the thousands.

The bulldozer's contribution to World War II is well documented. Thousands of crawler tractors, most carrying LeTourneau blades, or pulling LeTourneau scrapers, found their way overseas and to Alaska to prepare for other fighting forces. Bulldozers were often the first on the scene. They built air bases on islands across the South Pacific, as well as chains of bases across the Aleutian Islands toward Russia. They pushed the Alaska Highway through 1,400 miles of uncharted wilderness in just two summer seasons. Admiral William F. Halsey stated, "The four machines that won the war in the Pacific were the submarine, radar, the airplane, and the bulldozer."

Just after the war, Caterpillar replaced the popular 8R-series with the 2U-series D8 in late 1945. Nothing much changed on the tractor. It retained the same D13000 engine and the same 78-inch track gauge. Even the rated power of

113-drawbar horsepower and 132-belt horsepower remained the same for the initial machines. But from tractor No. 2U3532 (1947) these figures were upgraded to 130-drawbar horsepower and 148-belt horsepower. Sales of the 2U continued to forge ahead, and Caterpillar's largest tractor received slight modifications along the way. From tractor No. 2U5307 (1948) a forward-reverse lever was fitted; from tractor No. 2U11091 (1950) a two-position idler was available; from tractor No. 2U12283 (1950) it featured an enclosed clutch. Also in 1950, Caterpillar redesigned the radiator grill and front end to establish the look of the D8 for years to come. From tractor No. 2U21513 (1953) an oil clutch was standard. Some 23,537 2U-series tractors left the Peoria factory before production came to an end in 1953.

The final D8 tractor model based on the 1H-series design legacy, and powered by the D13000 engine, was the 13A series, in production from 1953 to 1955. Replacing the 2U, the 13A D8 received a power increase to 150-drawbar horsepower and 185-belt horsepower, but still no drastic changes in appearance. The "hard-nose" front was similar to that first seen on the former 2U tractor of 1950. The 13A was a popular tractor on large construction projects, and made an ideal companion to the Caterpillar No. 80 pull-type scraper with 17.5 cubic yards of heaped capacity.

The most successful D13000 engine was a real winner in every respect. Installed in Caterpillar's largest tractors since 1935 (1H, 8R, 2U, and 13A), it had carried Caterpillar through the war years and enabled the company to supply trouble-free engines in thousands of tractors on short notice without further testing or research. With a governed speed at full load of 1,000 rpm, the

engine ran slowly by today's standards, but there are those who say that this slow speed contributed to the engine's long operating life. And there are many D13000 engines, over 50 years old, still operational today. Those who have driven a D13000-equipped tractor, or stood by one pulling a scraper collecting a heaped load of dirt, will be familiar with the unique ground-vibrating throb of this powerful, low-revving diesel.

After 3,703 13A tractors had been shipped, Caterpillar finally made some major changes to its long-running D8 series in 1955. They launched two new versions that year, the D8D (15A-series) equipped with a torque converter, and the D8E (14A-series) with direct drive. Both of these

D7
This Caterpillar 3T-series D7 from June 1946 is equipped with a No. 7S straight bulldozer blade and No. 46 Hydraulic Control. This type of blade control was also available for the No. 7A angle bulldozer as well. *ECO Collection*

tractors were equipped with the Caterpillar D342, six-cylinder 5-3/4x8-inch bore-and-stroke diesel engine developing 155- drawbar horsepower and 191-flywheel horsepower. Their undercarriages boasted seven track rollers and hydraulic track adjusters. These two tractors lasted only a year in production when the D8D became the D8G, and the D8E became the D8F, both featuring oil-cooled brakes and clutches. The serial number prefixes did not change on these two tractors, but the model changes occurred with tractors 14A3861 and 15A1673, respectively.

Along with the RD8 introduced in 1935, Caterpillar began production of two other series of tractors that would follow a similar pattern of success. One of these, the RD6 (5E8501-series), was similar in design to the Diesel Forty. It carried the same D6100 engine, but was rated a little higher in power. After only five tractors were produced in the 5E series, a new-version RD6 (2H-series) came out that same year. This machine featured the Caterpillar D6600, three-cylinder 5-3/4x8-inch bore-and-stroke diesel rated at 43-drawbar horsepower and 50-belt horsepower. As with the other RD-series models, the RD6 nomenclature was changed to D6 in late 1937, but the tractor remained unaltered except for a higher power rating to 45-drawbar horsepower and 52-belt horsepower beginning with tractor No. 2H3248, released in 1937. In fact, the outward appearance of the RD6 and D6 versions was the same, and all were offered with either 56-inch or 74-inch track gauges. Sales reached 8,966 units before the 2H was superseded in 1941.

Caterpillar presented two new D6 versions in 1941, the 4R-series with a 74-inch track gauge, and the 5R-series

with a 60-inch track gauge. Their appearance was different from previous models, featuring modern-looking curves around the front radiator. Both models were powered by the Caterpillar D4600, six-cylinder 4-1/4x5-1/2-inch bore-and-stroke engine rated at 55-drawbar horsepower and 65-belt horsepower. In 1943, Caterpillar produced a restricted run of 45 specially armored D6 (1T3001-series) tractors for military use. These were essentially 4R-series tractors, but fully enclosed with heavy armor plating. The 4R/5R series continued in production until 1947 when a total of 9,148 had been shipped. They were replaced by a new D6 model, the 8U/9U series with track gauges of 60 inches and 74 inches, respectively.

Caterpillar installed its D318, six-cylinder diesel engine in the 8U and 9U D6 tractors. With a bore and stroke of 4-1/2x5-1/2 inches, it developed 66-drawbar horsepower and 76-belt horsepower. The 8U/9U tractor's appearance was changed again to a more conservative look—less rounded than the former model. The 8U and 9U D6 models stayed in Caterpillar's production line until 1959, and proved to be big sellers for the company. Over the years they received several minor design changes. From 1953, an oil clutch became standard; from tractors numbered 8U7662 and 9U16537 (1954), power was increased to 75-drawbar horsepower and 85-belt horsepower; from tractors numbered 8U10785 and 9U28328 (1959), the undercarriage featured hydraulic track adjusters.

The third new tractor Caterpillar released in 1935 was the RD7 (5E7501-series), and its development stages followed closely that of the RD6/D6. Of similar design to the Diesel Fifty, it carried the same D7700

RD6

In 1935, Caterpillar replaced its Diesel Forty with the RD6 model line. The first 5E8501-series of this tractor was basically a more powerful version of its predecessor. Only five were built. In that same year, it was replaced by a far more refined 2H-series RD6 featuring a Cat D6600, three-cylinder 5-3/4x8-inch bore-and-stroke diesel motor. All RD6 models were offered in 56- and 74-inch track gauges. The RD6 became the D6 in late 1937. This pristine wide-gauge RD6 (S.N. 2H221W) is a 1935 vintage tractor, restored by Dave Smith of Oregon. Today, this tractor is on permanent display at Caterpillar's East Peoria CV Building. Owner: Caterpillar, Inc. *Daniel's Photography/Dave Smith*

HIGH-SPEED D6

During 1942 and 1943, Caterpillar produced two tractor models referred to as High-Speed D6/D7 Heavy Tractor M1, to be used with towed artillery and cargo carriers. Both models featured transmission gears and engine governors with increased rpm settings, which enabled the tractors to travel at 11 miles per hour. Pictured is the High-Speed D6 model with a D4600 diesel engine, front-mounted Hyster winch, extended frame, and extended operator's deck. Approximately 453 of the D6 tractors were produced. There is no record of how many of the D7 variation were built. *ECO Collection*

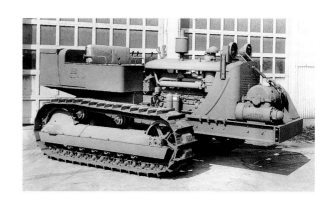

D5

In 1939, Caterpillar built a special tractor model identified as the D5 (S.N. prefix 9M). This D5 was essentially a D6 tractor fitted with a D4 undercarriage, with five track rollers and a 60-inch track gauge. The 9M-series D5 was powered by a Cat D4600, six-cylinder 4-1/4x5-1/2-inch bore-and-stroke diesel engine. Only 46 tractors were manufactured. Pictured is an ultra-rare 1939 D5 (S.N. 9M28). Owner: Paul Kirsch. *ECO*

engine but with a little more power. After only 25 5E-series tractors were built, it was replaced with a new-version RD7 (9G-series) that same year. The new machine featured the Caterpillar D8800, four-cylinder 5-3/4x8-inch bore-and-stroke diesel engine rated at 61-drawbar horsepower and 70-belt horsepower. In late 1937 the RD7 nomenclature was changed to D7, as with the other RD-series models, but the tractor remained the same. The early RD7 and D7 tractors were produced with a 60-inch track gauge, but from tractor No. 9G2508 (1937), a 74-inch gauge option was offered. Sales of the 9G-series amounted to 7,254 units before it was replaced by the D7 (7M-series) in 1940.

The D7 7M-series featured the rounded-front radiator and hood sheet metal found on the D6 of the same vintage, and was only offered with a 74-inch track gauge. The same D8800 engine powered this new D7, but its ratings were increased to 75-drawbar horsepower and 87-belt horsepower. By the end of 1940, these ratings were increased to 80 and

D4

The Caterpillar D4 model evolved from the 4G-series RD4 in late 1937. The 4G-series D4 would stay in production through 1938, with 9,999 manufactured, including RD4 models. It was replaced in 1939 by the 7J-series, which stayed in production until 1942, with another 9,999 built. Its replacement was the 2T-series D4 from 1943, which ended its run in 1945, again with 9,999 units. Pictured is an original 1945 military issue, narrow-gauge D4 (S.N. 5T1886). The 5T-series was in production from 1945 to 1947, with 7,411 tractors built. Owner: Ed Akin. *ECO*

D4 "ORCHARD"

The early Caterpillar RD4/D4 models were powered by the Cat D4400, four-cylinder 4-1/4x5-1/2-inch bore-and-stroke diesel engine. This engine would eventually be replaced by the Cat D315 diesel in 1947, with the introduction of the 6U- and 7U-series tractors. This immaculate D4 tractor is a 1937 wide-gauge "orchard" tailseat model (S.N. 4G8237W). *ECO*

D4

The D4 model line was an extremely popular tractor for Caterpillar. The D4 was big enough for large fieldwork, as well as a perfectly sized machine for the small to medium-sized contractor. This D4 (S.N. 7U36267) is a 1956 vintage wide-gauge machine equipped with the optional front-mounted No. 44 Hydraulic Control. Powerplant in this model was the D315, four-cylinder, 4-1/2x5-1/2-inch bore-and-stroke diesel engine. Owner: Brent Smith. *ECO*

90 horsepower, respectively. The 7M series was produced up to 1944, by which time 9,999 were made. It was superseded by the D7 (3T-series), which had a very similar appearance to its predecessor. It carried the same four-cylinder D8800 diesel, but received some mechanical refinements like a forward-reverse lever. From tractor No. 3T19863 (1952), a two-position idler was fitted; from tractor 3T23647 (1953), an oil

clutch became standard; and a boost in power occurred from tractor No. 3T25310 (1954) to 90-drawbar horsepower and 108-belt horsepower.

Along with the D8 already mentioned, the D7-size tractor also proved a favorite with the military during and immediately after World War II. It was a handy size to move around, could fit inside a small landing craft, yet when

D4 "ORCHARD"
All of the early Caterpillar RD4/D4 model series from the late 1930s, through the late 1950s, were available in 44-inch narrow-gauge and 60-inch wide-gauge track configurations. This wide-gauge 1937 "orchard" model D4 (S.N. 4G8237W) is equipped with the tailseat and rounded fender option, as well as front track-mounted "check breakers" for plowing through irrigation ridges in orchards. *ECO*

called upon to do major dirt moving with bulldozer or scraper, it came through with flying colors. In 1943 a special run of armored D7 (1T1001-series) tractors was built for military use. These were essentially 7M-series tractors, but fully enclosed with heavy armor plating. Only 138 of these special tractors were built. During 1944 and 1945, Caterpillar produced two more special military-version tractor models ordered by the Army Corps of Engineers. These were the 4T series, built from 1944 to 1945, and the 6T series, built only in 1945.

Caterpillar was so busy fulfilling these military orders that it sought some outside help. The company thus entered into an agreement with the American Car and Foundry Company of Berwick, Pennsylvania, to assemble large numbers of the 4T D7 tractor under license. The 4T and 6T were based on the standard 3T tractors at the time, but had special mechanical changes believed necessary by the Corps to enable them to withstand long-distance shipping and the harsh working environments they were likely

to experience in overseas operations. Many thousands of these military tractors were shipped around the world during the short two-year time frame. At the same time, D7 3T production stormed ahead. From 1940 through 1950, 36,545 D7 tractors of all models were shipped. And a further 12,703 D7 3T models were shipped up to 1955, when the production run ended.

The D7 3T model's replacement was known as the D7C (17A-series), which appeared in 1955. The redesigned tractor incorporated several changes and improvements, most important being its new D339 diesel engine. Rated at 102-drawbar horsepower and 128-belt horsepower, this engine had four cylinders of 5-3/4x8-inch bore and stroke. Retaining its 74-inch track gauge, the undercarriage now featured hydraulic track adjusters. Caterpillar continued to manufacture the D7C until it was replaced by the D7D in early 1959. The D7D featured oil-cooled brakes and steering clutches. A turbocharger was fitted to the engine, which produced 112-drawbar horsepower and 140-belt

D2

The D2 model line was the smallest diesel-powered crawler tractor to be manufactured by Caterpillar. First introduced in 1938 in the 3J-series (40-inch gauge) and the 5J-series (50-inch gauge), it was an instant hit with farmers. It was small enough to work between orchard rows, as well as large enough for open field disking and plowing duties. The early 3J- and 5J-series D2 tractors were powered by the Cat D3400, four-cylinder 3-3/4x5-inch bore-and-stroke engine. Pictured is a 1939 vintage D2 (S.N. 3J3433 SP) with left-side-mounted fuel tank. Owner: Tom Novak. *ECO*

D2

In 1947, Caterpillar introduced the 4U (40-inch gauge) and 5U (50-inch gauge) D2 tractors. The 4U/5U-series were powered by the Cat D311, four-cylinder, 4x5-inch bore-and-stroke diesel engine. Pictured in 2000 is a perfectly restored, 1952 wide-gauge D2 (5U9542) with left-side mounted fuel tank. Owner: Kent Bates. *ECO*

D2

This Caterpillar D2 (S.N. 5U15493) is a 1955 vintage model year tractor equipped with the rear-seat mounted fuel tank, extra wide trackshoes, 50-inch track gauge, full lighting package, and factory direct electric start. Owner: Dave Smith. *ECO*

D2 "ORCHARD"
The Caterpillar D2 was also offered in an "orchard" tailseat configuration for working around low-hanging tree branches. This D2 is a 1950 wide-gauge orchard model, carrying serial No. 5U5955. Production on the D2 model line would end in 1957 on both the 4U- and 5U-series tractors. *ECO*

horsepower. The 17A serial number prefix was allocated to the entire production runs of the D7C and D7D models.

After Caterpillar revamped its largest diesel tractor models in 1935, and established the D6, D7, and D8 family lines, it shifted focus to its smaller tractors. The company began to retire its older gasoline-powered tractors in favor of new diesel-powered designs. First was the RD4 (4G-series), which was introduced in 1936. The RD4 was similar to the R4 gasoline tractor and ran on the same 60-inch gauge undercarriage. Powered by a Caterpillar D4400, four-cylinder 4-1/4x5-1/2-inch bore-and-stroke diesel, it developed 35-drawbar horsepower and 41-belt horsepower. Like other tractors in the RD-series, the R was dropped in 1937, and the tractor continued as the D4, with a couple of minor design changes. The radiator was modified, and one carrier roller on each track frame was used instead of two. Caterpillar continued building the 4G D4 model until 1938, selling a total of 9,999 units.

After the 4G series, Caterpillar changed very little on the next three D4 tractor models that were produced up to 1947. The 7J series ran from 1939 to 1942, the 2T series from 1943 to 1945, and the 5T series from 1945 to 1947. All these tractors were powered by the Caterpillar D4400 diesel engine, and all offered a 44-inch or 60-inch track gauge. Power ratings remained virtually unchanged since the RD4's inception in 1936. This series of D4 tractors was extremely reliable and sold in huge numbers to contractors, farmers, and to the military. Collectively, the 7J, 2T, and 5T versions of the D4 chalked up an impressive sales count of 27,409 units.

In 1947, Caterpillar presented two new versions of its popular D4 tractor. The 6U (44-inch gauge) and 7U (60-inch gauge) were equipped with the D315, four-cylinder 4-1/2x5-1/2-inch bore-and-stroke diesel engine rated at 43-drawbar horsepower and 48-belt horsepower. With the new engine and other refinements on the 6U/7U D4

D4
The front-mounted Caterpillar No. 44 Hydraulic Control could be used to operate various Cat designed attachments, such as the No. 42 and No. 64 Tool Bar, the No. 4S and No. 4A Bulldozers, as well as the hydraulic controlled No. 40 towed scraper unit. The heavy-duty grille not only protected the radiator core, but also the hydraulic pump and reservoir tank. This D4 is a vintage 1956 7U-series, which was built from 1947 to 1959. Owner: Brent Smith. *ECO*

D2 "TRAXCAVATOR"
The Caterpillar D2 could be equipped with the Trackson "Traxcavator" T2 front-mounted, 3/4-cubic yard shovel attachment. Pictured is a 1948 vintage D2 (S.N. 5U1797) with the optional T2 Trackson loader. In December 1951 this combination became the Caterpillar T2 (S.N. prefix 31C) after Cat purchased the Trackson Company. Total Trackson T2/D2 combinations amounted to 1,604 units, while only 57 of the Caterpillar 31C-series T2 tractor-shovels were manufactured between 1952 and 1953. Owner: Historical Construction Equipment Association. *ECO*

EXPERIMENTAL D9 CONCEPT
This rather odd-looking concept Caterpillar crawler tractor from September 1946 is actually the starting point in the design evolution of the D9 tractor series. At this time, the prototype was equipped with rear-mounted radiators, which would soon be dropped from the design. The development of the D9 series would be hampered by lack of suitable machine tools able to handle components of the size the tractor would eventually require. *courtesy of Caterpillar, Inc. Corporate Archives*

tractors, Caterpillar had improved on what many believed was already perfection in the former long-running D4 series. Caterpillar continued production of the 6U/7U series right up to 1959, adding further design refinements along the way. From tractor numbers 6U10322 and 7U29424 (1954), power was increased to 48- drawbar horsepower and 54-belt horsepower. From tractor numbers 6U10363 and 7U29754 (1954), an oil clutch was offered. Then power was increased again from tractor numbers 6U11582 and 7U37285 (1956) to 50-drawbar horsepower and 57-belt horsepower. Over their long production runs at the Peoria plant, these D4 tractors racked up impressive sales. Farmers as well as contractors could afford this popular little tractor, and its market overlapped into many different industries from logging and mining, to oilfield work, pipelining, and landscaping. Most of the smaller Caterpillar tractors were available as "orchard specials," and the D4 was no exception. The D4 Orchard featured a low-slung cantilevered seat at the rear,

typical of other orchard tractors. By the time the D4 U-series production run ended in 1959, the 6U sales total ran to 12,781 units, while the 7U achieved a whopping 44,307 unit sales.

In 1938, Caterpillar introduced its smallest diesel tractor, the D2. Offered in two versions, the 3J (40-inch track gauge) and 5J (50-inch track gauge), the D2 was designed as a small, economical tractor intended to continue in the tradition of the company's past farm tractors. It certainly lived up to that tradition—and more. It turned out to be a very reliable, low-cost machine to operate, and although targeted for the agricultural market, the D2 followed in the footsteps of the D4, and found its way into a wide variety of applications ranging from small landscape contracting to surface coal mining. The 3J and 5J carried the Caterpillar D3400, four-cylinder 3 3/4 x 5-inch bore-and-stroke diesel engine rated at 25.5-drawbar horsepower and 31.5-belt horsepower. The D2 3J/5J series continued right through World War II and up to 1947, but none were manufactured in 1943. Sales totaled 19,161 units.

D9X

Pictured in April 1954 is the first pilot D9X crawler tractor built. This machine, which was one of 10 such tractors fabricated, was tested extensively in the field in all sorts of dozing conditions. At the time, these prototype D9X tractors were not equipped with a turbocharged engine. *Courtesy Caterpillar, Inc. Corporate Archives*

In 1947 the D2 received a major upgrade. The 3J became the 4U, and the 5J became the 5U, both tractors retaining their respective gauges of 40 inches and 50 inches. The radiator housing was altered from the previous design, but the big change was a new diesel engine under the hood. This was the Caterpillar D311, four-cylinder 4x5-inch bore-and-stroke diesel, giving the D2 32-drawbar horsepower and 38-belt horsepower. As with other long-running models, Caterpillar incorporated product improvements from time to time. From tractor numbers 4U5010 and 5U9814 (1952), power was increased to 35-drawbar horsepower and 39-belt horsepower. Then the D2 received another power increase from tractor numbers 4U6655 and 5U14551 (1954) to 38-drawbar horsepower and 43-belt horsepower. From tractor numbers 4U7020 and 5U16128 (1955), an oil clutch was made available. After sales of 26,454 units, Caterpillar discontinued the D2 in 1957, and built no more tractors of this size.

Caterpillar launched an intermediate-size tractor in 1939 known as the D5 (9M-series). This model was intended to fit between the well-established D6/D7/D8 tractors at the top end of the product line, and the D2/D4 tractor lines at the lower end of the scale. The D5 was equipped with the Caterpillar D4600, six-cylinder 4-1/4x5-1/2-inch bore-and-stroke diesel engine rated at 45-drawbar horsepower and 52-belt horsepower. It was a kind of hybrid D4 and D6 tractor, possessing the undercarriage of the former and the main frame of the latter. But the D5 did not stay long in production. After one special production run of 46 tractors, Caterpillar pulled it from the line. The D5 nomenclature did not reappear until some 28 years later when Caterpillar launched an entirely different D5 tractor in 1967.

POSTWAR EXPANSION

The recession that occurred following World War I was not repeated following World War II, and most manufacturing companies like Caterpillar were able to convert from military to civilian production relatively smoothly. Lessons learned from the previous postwar depression, still within memory, enabled the companies and the U.S. Government to take affirmative action. The government did not return large quantities of product to the manufacturers and did not cancel major orders. Thousands of tractors were left behind when the military vacated the South Pacific islands, and many more were simply dumped overboard from transport ships. This extremely wasteful action did, however, boost the economy for replacement equipment that was needed to rebuild Europe, and for machines to continue with the many North American projects postponed during the war years. For Caterpillar, the excess manufacturing capacity generated by the cessation of government orders was soon filled with new products. In fact, by the end of 1946, backlog orders were at an all-time high for the company.

Toward the end of World War II, and in the immediate succeeding years, several events occurred causing a major change in the earthmoving equipment manufacturing industry. Up to this time, tractor manufacturers were not interested in making the working attachments for their tractors. They favored leaving this important market segment to specialist companies—who made the rippers, blades, scrapers, and other attachments. As military orders declined after the war, tractor makers found themselves with excess manufacturing space that needed to be filled. So most introduced their own brands of tractor attachments manufactured in-house, and broke off the alliances forged earlier with the specialist companies. Although alliances were broken, the main-line tractor builders' move to manufacturing their own tractor attachments did not put the specialist companies out of business. There was still a good market for even more specialist tractor attachments, and many new entrants to the auxiliary equipment industry have sprung up over the years since the war.

Typical of most manufacturers toward the end of World War II, Caterpillar foresaw the problem of excess manufacturing capability, but the company had to deal with another more pressing issue. Back in 1938, R.G. LeTourneau introduced the world's first self-propelled, rubber-tired scraper known as the Tournapull. LeTourneau probably didn't know it at the time, but the Tournapull marked the start of high-speed earthmoving. Caterpillar watched this development with intense interest, and in 1941 brought out its own high-speed rubber-tired tractor, the DW-10, designed for pulling scrapers and wagons. With the two earthmoving equipment giants now competing for the same market segment, the distribution agreement between Caterpillar and LeTourneau established in 1934 became strained. It just didn't make sense to Caterpillar that their dealers should distribute products from another company that made products competing with their own, even though the LeTourneau scraper did utilize a Caterpillar engine. So in February 1944, after months of speculation, LeTourneau officially announced that the alliance between the two companies would be discontinued immediately. Then in May 1944, Caterpillar announced it was going to start production of its own allied tractor equipment and soon brought out a range of bulldozer blades, pull-scrapers, rippers, and PCUs.

First came a line of PCUs and cable-operated straight dozer blades in 1945, followed by angling blades a year later. Then in 1947, hydraulically operated dozer blades appeared. Caterpillar launched its first line of pull-scrapers in 1946. These were the No. 60 (7.5 cubic yards heaped), No. 70 (11 cubic yards heaped), and No. 80 (17.5 cubic yards heaped), which were tailor-made for the D6, D7, and D8 tractors, respectively. Later in 1949, the No. 40 hydraulic scraper (4.5 cubic yards heaped) was presented for use with the D4 tractor. A larger No. 90 (27 cubic yards heaped) came out in 1951. But Caterpillar's largest tractor at the time was still the D8, so that is what pulled the No. 90 until the D9 was launched in 1955.

One company not affected by Caterpillar's postwar decision to build their own tractor equipment was the Trackson Company—at least not for the time being. The Trackson Company of Milwaukee, Wisconsin, had been building cable-operated pipelaying attachments for Caterpillar tractors since 1936. In 1937, Trackson began supplying Caterpillar with vertical-lift cable-operated loader attachments for its tractors. The first of these was mounted on a Caterpillar Thirty (6G) tractor. Subsequently the company developed a line of loaders specifically matched to the Caterpillar D2, D4, D6, and D7 crawler tractors and called them "Traxcavators." The Trackson attachment consisted of a heavy frame mounted over and above the tractor hood. The frame supported the hoisting sheaves and bucket arms as well as a cable winch driven from the tractor's front PTO. The Traxcavator models were the T2, T4, T6, and T7, which matched their respective tractor models with bucket capacities ranging from 1/2 cubic yard for the T2 to 2 cubic yards for the T7.

By 1950, Trackson added hydraulics to its loaders, the first being mounted on a modified D4, and known as the model HT4. This hydraulic loader design was a real breakthrough. Gone were the complicated cables, winches, and mechanical linkages. In their place was a neat two-motion hydraulically powered linkage, and two levers controlling hoist and bucket tilt. Most importantly, the heavy frame

D9D

In 1955, Caterpillar officially released the big D9D for sale. The D9D was offered in two model series types: the 18A-series with direct drive and the 19A-series with torque converter drive. Power was supplied by a Cat D353, six-cylinder 6-1/4x8-inch bore-and-stroke turbocharged diesel engine. Both the 18A- and 19A-series D9D machines would end production in 1959. Pictured is a 1955 18A-series D9D crawler that just happens to be the very first unit to have been sold in Oregon. It is equipped with a No. 9A Bulldozer and No. 30 Cable Control, and upper engine guard. Owner: The Halton Company. *ECO*

and top-heavy draw works previously mounted high above the engine hood had been eliminated. The result was a nimble, lighter, and more-productive machine with vastly enhanced stability. Caterpillar looked so favorably on this new design that it purchased the Trackson Company outright in December 1951, and adopted the Traxcavator name for its crawler loaders. Trackson's former loader and pipelayer models were incorporated into Caterpillar's product line. The crawler loader models were Traxcavators T2 (31C-series), T4 (32C-series), T6 (33C-series), T7 (34-series), as well as TracLoaders L2 (36C-series) and LW2 (37C-series). The pipelayer models included the PD4 (38C-series), MD6 (39C-series), MD7 (40C-series), MD8 (41C-series), and the MDW8 (42C-series). The last machine featured a hydraulically moveable counterweight.

But the Trackson-designed crawler loaders experienced a short life as Caterpillar machines. The T-series disappeared within a year with less than 100 produced for each model. The L2 and LW2 lasted until 1953, but the well-liked 1-1/4-yard HT4 (35C-series) loader continued in Caterpillar's product line until 1955. The pipelayers continued in production and became the forerunners of the present-day machines.

With experience gained on crawler loaders in the previous decade, tractor manufacturers in the early 1950s began to realize that the crawler loader, as well as bulldozers, had to be designed from the ground up. It was not sufficient simply to hang the loader arms and bucket on a standard crawler tractor. The loader needed proper balance, with a frame designed for the rigors of heavy excavating. So by the mid-1950s, crawler loaders and bulldozers were no longer a tractor with an attachment. They were an integrated unit, designed for production as a dozer from the ground up. The old Trackson designs were phased out, and Caterpillar launched its first integrated hydraulic crawler loader, the No. 6 Traxcavator (10A-series) in 1953. Based on the D6 9U tractor, but with a modified frame and longer seven-roller undercarriage, the No. 6 carried a 2-yard bucket. Two years later, the No. 6 was phased out to make way for Caterpillar's new line of Traxcavators. The first of these, the 955C (12A-series) with bucket capacity of 1-1/2

D9D
The Caterpillar D9 crawler tractor series would be the face of dozing power in the earth-moving industry for years to come. Although a few other manufacturers tried to counter the big D9, all would take a back seat to this tractor in performance and reliability. The early D9D models utilized either a rear-mounted No. 29 Cable Control or a front-mounted No. 30 unit (pictured). With the introduction of the D9E model series in 1959, a new front-mounted No. 184 Hydraulic Control was also made available. Owner: The Halton Company. *ECO*

cubic yards, was announced early in 1955. By the end of that year, the 933C (11A-series) and 977D (20A-series) were added, giving the company a three-machine range of crawler loaders from 1 to 2-1/4 cubic yards.

After the end of World War II, Caterpillar continued to sell its crawler tractors in large numbers even though military orders had diminished. The agricultural market remained steady, but the real increase came from the construction market. A war-torn Europe needed rebuilding. Roads, bridges, harbors, and most other infrastructure required much-needed

maintenance postponed and further damaged while nations were at war. Major civilian projects that had been on the drawing boards since before the war were now being released for commencement, and surface mining for much-needed minerals and coal was expanding rapidly. Caterpillar's development policy was to keep a close watch on all of the industries using its products and to satisfy the needs of contractors who, it seemed, always wanted to move more earth in a shorter time, and at a lower cost. With the rapidly increasing size of earthmoving projects around the world, Caterpillar foresaw the need for larger equipment and, in typical company fashion, started experimental work behind the scenes on a crawler tractor much larger than anything previously built by Caterpillar or any of its competitors.

The legendary D9 was officially announced for sale in mid-1955, but its development can be traced as far back as 1946 when Caterpillar engineers started to experiment with a prototype tractor more powerful than the D8. This one-off machine featured many radical concepts, including an offset operator's station mounted above the left track and radiators mounted at the rear. The hood was sloped on both sides to form a peak at the top, and combined with the rear-mounted radiator, operator visibility was unprecedented. But Caterpillar management decided that this design was too radical to put into production, and took a more conservative approach with future designs. Another important consideration was how to mass-produce a larger tractor than had ever been built before. It was the same problem faced by any company pushing technology to the limits. And back in the 1940s, manufacturing systems to economically produce a machine the size of the D9 were still in their infancy.

During the early 1950s, Caterpillar pursued its large tractor program over several phases. First, new larger components were tested and monitored on special D8 tractors. Then in 1952, it constructed two experimental tractors that would form the basis of the future D9 design. These units were monitored over a two-year period at Caterpillar's proving ground, and the results obtained enabled the big tractor program to proceed to the next phase of testing. In 1954, Caterpillar built 10 more test tractors, completely redesigned based on the knowledge gained from the previous tests. These tractors, known as D9X models, were sent to select locations across the country to be

exposed to a variety of real site conditions. Others continued extensive testing at the proving grounds. All of these tractors were monitored closely, and their operators were quizzed for their opinions on power, maneuverability, responsiveness, and ease of operation. Maintenance personnel were similarly interviewed for opinions on ease of maintenance and accessibility.

One of the design innovations added to the D9 before final launch was a turbocharger. The engine installed in the D9X tractor was the new D353, six-cylinder 6-1/4x8-inch bore-and-stroke diesel rated at approximately 200-flywheel horsepower. Reports from the field indicated that the tractor appeared under-powered for its weight, so Caterpillar engineers installed a turbocharger to boost the power.

At last the D9 was ready for mass production in mid-1955, and the first commercial version was known as the D9D. It was offered in two versions, both with a 90-inch track gauge. The 18A-series had a direct drive transmission, and the 19A-series was equipped with a torque converter. The D353 turbocharged engine was rated at 230-drawbar horsepower and 286-flywheel horsepower for the first series of tractors. However, the year after the D9D's introduction, power ratings were increased to 260-drawbar horsepower and 320-flywheel horsepower. This occurred from tractor numbers 18A1065 and 19A654. Caterpillar produced the D9D in this same format until 1959, when it was replaced by the D9E series.

With its powerful and versatile machines, and commitment to advanced technology, Caterpillar made important contributions not just to agriculture, but to earthmoving and construction projects around the world. Whether it was a new design, or a new size, Caterpillar management and engineers anticipated the needs and opportunities of the postwar years, making the company a pivotal international presence in the heavy equipment industry.

Although the scope of this book details Caterpillar's crawler tractor development from inception to 1955, no Caterpillar history book would be complete without an overview of the tremendous advancements and progress achieved in the 46 years since then, and an appreciation of how large the company has grown. As far as crawler tractors are concerned, Caterpillar stayed at the forefront of development, and although not boasting any world record holders in crawler tractor size, it kept pace with market demands.

Each crawler tractor in Caterpillar's line has received constant updates over the years. These improvements have usually meant increased horsepower, better fuel economy, and more comfort and ease of operation for the operator. Some of the most notable crawler tractors included the D8H. Unveiled in 1958 with 235-flywheel horsepower, the D8H went on to becoming one of Caterpillar's best-selling large tractors. It received a power boost to 270-flywheel horsepower in late 1965, and remained in the line until it was replaced by the D8K in 1974. The famous D9 was never the biggest tractor in the world, but as Caterpillar's largest until 1977, it earned the reputation of being the most reliable big tractor in the field, and the mainstay of large earthmoving projects and surface mining operations. It progressed through the D, E, G, and H models, and by the

D11R
The Caterpillar D11R model series is the largest, most powerful, and productive crawler tractor the company has ever produced. With 850-flywheel horsepower available from its Cat 3508B EUI diesel engine, the D11R can take on the largest dozing assignments imaginable. *ECO*

117

CHALLENGER 95E
The Challenger 95E is the most powerful Mobil-trac System (MTS) ag tractor manufactured by Caterpillar. Developing 410-gross horsepower, it can handle big field jobs formerly reserved for large rubber-tired, four-wheel-drive, articulated tractors. Low ground compaction is the name of the game with the rubber-tracked MTS Challengers. Although the 95E is a large and powerful tractor, it "treads" lightly wherever it goes. *ECO*

time the D9H was superseded in 1980, power had increased to 410 flywheel horsepower. A new-size model emerged in 1967 in the form of the 93-flywheel horse-power D5. This model became one of Caterpillar's most versatile mid-sized tractors with many variations offered.

Caterpillar's big breakthrough came in 1977 with the unveiling of the "high-drive" tractor—the first D10. Caterpillar's elevated sprocket design had a long and inter-esting development period going back as far as 1969. Engineers tested many ideas and concepts before building the first prototype in 1973. The high-drive sprocket meant that uneven ground shocks were absorbed by a cushioned undercarriage instead of the drive axle, and the drivetrain was raised out of the mud. These advantages translated into operator comfort, ease of servicing, and lower repair costs. The elevated sprocket idea was not new, as several manufacturers had marketed tractors with this drive con-cept in the early days of tractor development. All of these

had been discontinued decades earlier, so it was a daring move on Caterpillar's part to reinvent the design on the D10. This totally new concept was about to change Caterpillar's entire line of large crawler tractors, the big moneymakers. The D10, at 700 horsepower, and weighing 88 tons with blade, was by far Caterpillar's heaviest and most powerful tractor up to that time. It caused a lot of apprehension at first. The big question was, how can the drive sprocket exert its full power without jumping out of engagement, with such a reduced circumference in contact with the track pins? Caterpillar's answer was twofold: the tracks must be adjusted to the correct tension, and the state-of-the-art sealed and lubricated tracks would all but eliminate stretch.

The gamble paid off handsomely for Caterpillar. Nearly a thousand D10s were sold until the 770-horse-power D11N replaced it in 1986. By that time, the high-drive design had expanded to all its tractors down to the

D6H-size. Since then, high-drive versions of the D5 and D4 models have been built. Caterpillar's current crawler line includes "M" and "R" series tractors, spanning power ratings from 70- to 850-flywheel horsepower. The largest is the D11R CD (Carry-Dozer), which has a special 22-foot-wide curved blade, enabling it to move 20 to 30 percent more material than the standard D11R.

Through all this large crawler tractor development geared to the heavy construction and mining industries, Caterpillar never forgot its farming roots. Over the two decades since World War II, crawler tractors continued to sell to the agricultural market on a steady but continuous basis. Toward the end of the 1950s, Caterpillar strongly promoted its crawler tractors to farmers, even though it had dropped its smallest tractor, the D2, from the product line. Caterpillar literature at the time promoted the D4 and D6, which were equipped with tool bars for an array of farm implements. These included disc plows, cultivators, chisels, subsoilers, and special root plows for undercutting brush roots in dry areas. The D4 and D6 tractors were offered with the No. 4 and No. 6 tool bars attached to "Swing-Around" arms pivoted to the center of each crawler frame. When not pulling the tool bar, the arms could be swung around to the front of the tractor and used with a bulldozer blade.

Agricultural applications were not confined to small tractors. Some of the larger farms found good use for the D7 and D8-size tractors. They just hooked on more implements to get the job done faster. A typical operation might use a D7 pulling three five-bottom plows in third or fourth gear, and covering nine acres per hour, 6 inches deep—or a D8 pulling two heavy drills and disks, and covering 20 acres per hour. Some of the largest farms even employed D9s, especially where land clearing was involved. One D9 equipped with a tree cutter and V-dozer blade was reported clearing land in Arkansas. Felling trees averaging 18 inches in diameter, the big tractor maintained a pace of 15 acres per eight-hour day on the 3,500-acre clearing job to increase productive land.

In the 1960s, Caterpillar introduced Special Application (SA) versions of its smaller tractors. These are direct-drive tractors geared to suit farming operations demanding high-speed tillage. They feature a low center of gravity, and are balanced with their weight forward for drawbar work. Wider track shoes are available, and the SA tractor engines run at a higher speed, producing more flywheel horsepower than the standard versions. The D4C SA was unveiled in 1966 followed by the D5 SA a year later. The D6C SA joined the line in 1970. Since then, the SA adaptions have been applied to the D7-, and D8-series tractors.

To better reflect Caterpillar's diverse product line, the company changed its name in 1986 from Caterpillar Tractor Company to Caterpillar, Inc. That same year Caterpillar unveiled two different ranges of farm tractors for the agricultural market. The first was the AG6. Based on the D6, it boasted a longer main frame, and longer crawler frames. Its advanced hydraulic system was tailor-made for sustained drawbar work, featuring a large-volume hydraulic oil reservoir for cooling, and a fuel tank providing up to 14 hours of continuous operation. The driver's cab, positioned some 38 inches further forward than the D6, provided excellent balance for drawbar work. Inside the cab, the driver was treated to a maximum 85-decibles sound level, a multi-position swivel seat, and pressurized air conditioning. Although popular in the western United States, the AG6 was relatively short-lived as a Caterpillar product, and was withdrawn in 1993. An AG4 model based on the D4 was also briefly offered in 1986 but was soon dropped. Company records show that only seven AG4s were built, making this one of Caterpillar's rarest tractors.

The other line of agricultural tractors Caterpillar released in 1986 was far more successful. This was the Challenger series of rubber-tracked machines, which had been under development since 1979. Starting with a specially modified D4E SA tractor, several different power-trains were tested to ascertain the one most suitable for high-speed agricultural use. Another program fully evaluated the feasibility of a rubber-tracked undercarriage by experimenting with various rubber belt concepts on a special test bed in Caterpillar's research facility. These two programs were brought together in 1981 when a unit called the BAT mobile was tested. The BAT (Belted Agricultural Tractor) was the previous experimental D4E SA, now fitted with the rubber tracks. The next step was to fit rubber tracks on two converted D6D SA tractors. Beginning in 1983, these were run for thousands of hours, under closely monitored conditions, over a four-year period.

In 1984 the first two tractors built from the ground up as Challengers were ready for testing, and by 1985, further pre-production units were being field tested all over the United States. The lengthy pre-production program came to a close in late 1986 when Caterpillar released its first Challenger for sale. Full production of the 270-horsepower model 65 began the following year. The rubber-belted undercarriage, referred to by Caterpillar as the Mobil-trac System, consists of rubber belts reinforced with four layers of flexible steel cable. The rear driving wheels are also coated with a 2-inch rubber rim and drive the belts by friction. The tracks are kept in alignment by longitudinal lugs on the tracks running in grooves in the front idler and the rear drive wheel. The bogie-mounted mid rollers are air-suspended, and allow the crawler belts to float over uneven ground, providing the tractor with excellent traction as well as superior flotation to avoid getting stuck. At the same time, the much greater bearing area of the crawler tracks compared with that of similar-sized wheel tractors results in lower ground pressure and minimizes compaction to the soil, a very important consideration in modern farming practices. Caterpillar has gone to great lengths to extol the virtues of its farm crawlers over wheel tractors when soil compaction is considered. Detailed tests have proven that greater crop yields have resulted from the use of crawler tractors when compared with wheel tractors working in the same conditions. Over the past 15 years the Caterpillar Challenger tractor line has expanded to seven models ranging from 150- to 317-drawbar horsepower.

As if the expanded agricultural farm tractor line was not enough to prove Caterpillar was serious about being a major farm equipment supplier, the company re-entered the combine harvester business in 1997 when it announced a joint venture with the German firm Claas KgaA. Combines had been absent from Caterpillar's product line since 1935 when the company sold the licensing and manufacturing rights of the original Holt and Best machines to Deere & Company. The new venture allowed Claas combines to be sold and serviced in North America under the Caterpillar name, and the full range of Caterpillar's Challenger tractors to be sold in Europe under the Claas name.

In the years since 1955, the company has expanded into one of the world's largest manufacturing organizations, and the No. 1 company in construction and mining equipment. It has not only broadened its established lines with upgraded models as soon as technology or the market allowed, but has also introduced an extensive variety of new product lines reaching into many different industries. Back in 1955, Caterpillar's main products consisted of crawler tractors, crawler loaders, pipelayers, motor scrapers, pull-type scrapers, graders, and diesel engines. In 2001 those same seven product lines continued on a much broader scale, and they have been joined by an array of other products as summarized in Table 5.

Today, Caterpillar offers no less than 24 major product lines ranging from asphalt pavers to large mining shovels, from compact loaders to the world's largest trucks. The organization spans the globe with 42 manufacturing plants in the United States and another 49 plants strategically placed in 19 different countries.

BIBLIOGRAPHY

Reference was made to the following books and publications for additional background on Caterpillar, its people and its products:

Caterpillar, Inc. *Fifty Years on Tracks*. Caterpillar Tractor Company, Peoria, Illinois 1954.

Caterpillar, Inc. *The Caterpillar Story*. Caterpillar Tractor Company, Peoria, Illinois 1984.

Leffingwell, Randy. *Caterpillar Dozers and Tractors*. Motorbooks International, Osceola, Wisconsin 1994.

Wik, Reynold M. *Benjamin Holt & Caterpillar: Tracks and Combines*. American Society of Agricultural Engineers, St. Joseph, Michigan 1984.

Payne, Walter A. *Benjamin Holt: The Story of the Caterpillar Tractor*. University of the Pacific, Stockton, California, 1982.

Orlemann, Eric C. *Caterpillar Chronicle*. MBI Publishing Company, Osceola, Wisconsin 2000.

Haddock, Keith. *Giant Earthmovers an Illustrated History*. MBI Publishing Company, Osceola, Wisconsin 2000.

Lane, Michael R. *The Steam Plough Works*. Northgate Publishing Company, London, England 1980.

TABLES

TABLE 1: TILLER-WHEEL CRAWLER TRACTORS HOLT AND C.L. BEST

Make	Model	Series	Manufactured		At	No. Produced	Notes
			From	To			
Holt	Tracked Road Engine	—	1904		Stockton		First steam crawler built
Holt	Paddle Wheel Traction Engine	—	1906		Stockton		First steam crawler sold. No. 111
Holt	18 Midget	—	1914	1917	Stockton	347	
Holt	Baby 30	—	1912	1916	Stockton	301	
Holt	40	1001	1906	1909	Stockton	56	First gasoline crawler tractor
Holt	40	T-2	1913	1913	Peoria	72	
Holt	45B	—	1909	1909	Minneapolis	2	Built by Northern Holt Co.
Holt	45B	—	1909	1909	Winnipeg	2	Built by Canadian Holt Co.
Holt	45 (40-45)	—	1909	1911	Stockton	154	
Holt	45 (30-45)	T-1	1910	1913	Peoria	94	
Holt	60	T-7	1911	1915	Stockton	691	
Holt	60 (40-60)	T-4	1911	1916	Peoria	260	
Holt	75 (60-75)	A-NVS	1913	1916	Stockton	600	
Holt	75	T-6	1914	1915	Peoria	16	
Holt	75	—	1917	1918	Lincoln	442	Built by Ruston & Hornsby Ltd.
Holt	75	T-8	1916	1921	Stockton	1,377	
Holt	75	T-8	1915	1918	Peoria	2,118	
Holt	75	T-8	1921	1924	Stockton	67	Upgraded T-8
Holt	120	A-PEP	1914	1915	Peoria	Incl. below	Enclosed Peoria motor
Holt	120	T-9 (A-PLP)	1915	1922	Peoria	698	Ell-Head Peoria motor
C.L. Best	30 H.P. (Humpback)	—	1914	1915	Elmhurst	45	
C.L. Best	70 H.P. Tracklayer	—	1912	1914	Elmhurst	Incl. below	First Best crawler
C.L. Best	75 H.P. Tracklayer	—	1914	1919	Elmhurst	734	Build starts mid-1916 San Leandro
C.L. Best	90 H.P. Tracklayer	—	1916	1917	San Leandro	39	
C.L. Best	120 H.P. Tracklayer	—	1916	1917	San Leandro	5	

TABLE 2: NON-TILLER WHEEL CRAWLER TRACTOR HOLT & C.L. BEST

Make	Model	Series	Manufactured From	To	At	No. Produced	Notes
Holt	12	F-KEB	1916	1916	Peoria	1	Beaver motor
Holt	18 (12-18)	E-JEB	1915	1918	Peoria	3	Beaver motor
Holt	18	T-11A	1918	1918	Peoria	1	E-JEB with special track links
Holt	18	T-11B	1918	1918	Peoria	1	E-JEB with 8-cyl. Hershel-Spillman motor
Holt	20-30 (D-HTD)	T-5	1913	1913	Peoria	11	30 bhp
Holt	45	T-10	1915	1920	Stockton	1,239	
Holt	45 (D-HVS)	T-10	1914	1919	Peoria	610	165 tractors classified commercial domestic
Holt	45 (E-HVS)	T-12	1917	1918	Peoria	42	Armored Artillery Tractor
Holt	45 Long-Track (Military)	M1917	1917	1917	Peoria	1	No.20316 built with two different track designs
Holt	55 (10-Ton)	T-16	1917	1919	Peoria	2,103	Armored Artillery Tractor
Holt	55 (10-Ton)	T-16	1918	1919	Cleveland	700	As above but built by Chandler
Holt	120 Long-Track	T-24	1918	1918	Peoria	1	Military
Holt	2-Ton	T-35	1921	1924	Stockton	1,350	Riveted frame
Holt	2-Ton	T-35	1924	1925	Peoria	816	Cast-steel frame, became Cat. 2-Ton
Holt	2-1/2-Ton (Military)	T-13	1918	1918	Indianapolis	7	Built by Interstate Motor Co.
Holt	2-1/2-Ton (Military)	T-13	1918	1919	Detroit	87	Built by Federal Motor Truck Co
Holt	5-Ton (Military)	T-11	1917	1918	Detroit	2,193	Built by Maxwell
Holt	5-Ton (Military)	T-11	1917	1918	Lansing	1,477	Built by Reo
Holt	5-Ton (Military)	T-11	1917	1918	Peoria	3	
Holt	5-Ton (Commercial)	T-11	1919	1923	Peoria	2,425	Does not include renumbered units
Holt	5-Ton	T-29	1923	1924	Stockton	213	Riveted track frame
Holt	5-Ton (Experimental)	T-29	1921	1921	Peoria	6	
Holt	5-Ton (Experimental)	T-30	1921	1921	Peoria	1	Military T-29 S.N.11684
Holt	New 5-Ton	T-29	1924	1925	Peoria	353	Became Cat. 5-Ton
Holt	10-Ton	T-16	1918	1925	Peoria	3,028	Became Cat.10-Ton
Holt	10-Ton (Western)	TS-21	1921	1923	Stockton	152	
C.L. Best	16 H.P. Pony Tracklayer	8-16	1916	1917	San Leandro	3	
C.L. Best	25 H.P. Tracklayer	16-25	1918	1920	San Leandro	300	Replaced 1917 C.L.B. 30 H.P. Tracklayer
C.L. Best	30 H.P. Tracklayer	—	1917	1917	San Leandro	15	
C.L. Best	30 Tracklayer	S	1921	1925	San Leandro	Incl. w/Thirty	Became Cat. Thirty
C.L. Best	40 H.P. Tracklayer	—	1914	1919	San Leandro	747	
C.L. Best	45 H.P. Tracklayer	No. 190	1918	1918	San Leandro	1	
C.L. Best	60 Tracklayer	A	1919	1925	San Leandro	Incl. w/Sixty	Became Cat. Sixty

TABLE 3: CATERPILLAR GASOLINE CRAWLER TRACTORS—UP TO 1955

Model	Series	Manufactured From	To	At	No. Produced	Notes
2-Ton	T-35	1925	1928	Peoria	8,173	Originally Holt 2-ton
5-Ton	T-29	1925	1926	Peoria	1,147	Originally Holt 5-Ton
10-Ton	T-16	1925	1925	Peoria	454	Originally Holt 10-ton
Ten	PT	1928	1933	Peoria	4,932	395 high-clearance built
Fifteen	PV	1928	1932	Peoria	7,559	
Fifteen (Small)	7C	1932	1933	Peoria	307	Replaced Ten
Fifteen (Hi.Cl.)	1D	1932	1933	Peoria	95	Replaced Ten high-clearance
Twenty	L	1927	1929	San Leandro	1,970	
Twenty	PL	1928	1932	Peoria	6,331	
Twenty (Small)	8C	1932	1933	Peoria	652	Replaced Fifteen (PV)
Twenty-Two	2F	1934	1937	Peoria	9,999	Replaced Twenty (8C)
Twenty-Two	1J	1937	1939	Peoria	5,157	Replaced Twenty-Two (2F)
Twenty-Five	3C	1931	1933	Peoria	638	Replaced Twenty (PL)
Twenty-Eight	4F	1933	1935	Peoria	1,171	Replaced Twenty-Five
Thirty	S1001	1925	1930	San Leandro	9,445	Total includes Best 30
Thirty	PS	1926	1932	Peoria	14,294	
Thirty	6G	1935	1938	Peoria	Incl.with R-4	Became the R-4 in 1938
Thirty-Five	5C	1932	1935	Peoria	1,730	Replaced Thirty (PS)
Forty	5G	1934	1936	Peoria	584	Replaced Thirty-Five
Fifty	5A	1931	1937	Peoria	1,707	
Sixty	A	1925	1930	San Leandro	5,415	Total includes Best 60
Sixty	PA	1925	1931	Peoria	13,516	One built in 1932
Sixty-Five	2D	1932	1933	Peoria	521	Replaced Sixty
Seventy	8D	1933	1937	Peoria	266	
R-2	5E3501	1934	1937	Peoria	83	
R-2	4J	1938	1942	Peoria	1,185	40-inch gauge
R-2	6J	1938	1942	Peoria	1,150	50-inch gauge
R-3	5E2501	1934	1935	Peoria	60	
R-4	6G	1938	1944	Peoria	5,383	Total includes model Thirty 6G
R-5	5E3001	1934	1936	Peoria	500	
R-5	4H	1936	1940	Peoria	1,000	
R-5	3R	1940	1940	Peoria	49	
R-6	N/A	1941	1941	Peoria	N/A	Estimated 5 built, no confirmation

TABLE 4: CATERPILLAR DIESEL CRAWLER TRACTORS—UP TO 1955

Model	Series	Manufactured From	To	At	No. Produced	Notes
Diesel Thirty-Five	6E	1933	1934	Peoria	1,999	
Diesel Forty	3G	1934	1936	Peoria	1,971	Replaced Diesel Thirty-Five
Diesel Fifty	1E	1933	1936	Peoria	2,065	
Diesel Sixty	1C	1931	1931	San Leandro	2	First Cat. diesel
Diesel Sixty/Sixty-Five	1C	1931	1932	Peoria	155	
Diesel Seventy	3E	1933	1933	Peoria	51	
Diesel Seventy-Five	2E	1933	1935	Peoria	1,078	Replaced Diesel Seventy
D2	3J	1938	1947	Peoria	8,600	40-inch gauge
D2	5J	1938	1947	Peoria	10,561	50-inch gauge
D2	4U	1947	1957	Peoria	7,560	40-inch gauge
D2	5U	1947	1957	Peoria	18,894	50-inch gauge
RD4	4G	1936	1937	Peoria	Incl. below	
D4	4G	1937	1938	Peoria	9,999	Former RD4
D4	7J	1939	1942	Peoria	9,999	
D4	2T	1943	1945	Peoria	9,999	
D4	5T	1945	1947	Peoria	7,411	
D4	6U	1947	1959	Peoria	12,781	
D4	7U	1947	1959	Peoria	44,307	
D5	9M	1939	1939	Peoria	46	
RD6	5E8501	1935	1935	Peoria	5	Replaced Diesel Forty
RD6	2H	1935	1937	Peoria	Incl. below	
D6	2H	1937	1941	Peoria	8,966	Former RD6
D6	4R	1941	1947	Peoria	3,633	74-inch gauge
D6	5R	1941	1947	Peoria	5,515	60-inch gauge
D6A (Armored))	1T3001	1943	1943	Peoria	45	
D6 Hi-Speed (Military)	N/A	1942	1943	Peoria	453	Artillery tractor
D6	8U	1947	1959	Peoria	11,045	60-inch gauge
D6	9U	1947	1959	Peoria	29,764	74-inch gauge
D6 (Military)	9A700	1947	N/A	Peoria	N/A	
RD7	5E7501	1935	1935	Peoria	25	Replaced Diesel Fifty
RD7	9G	1935	1937	Peoria	Incl. below	
D7	9G	1937	1940	Peoria	7,254	Former RD7
D7	7M	1940	1944	Peoria	9,999	
D7A (Armored)	1T1001	1943	1943	Peoria	138	
D7 Hi-Speed (Military)	N/A	1942	1943	Peoria	N/A	Artillery tractor
D7	3T	1944	1955	Peoria	28,058	
D7 (Military)	4T	1944	1945	Peoria	9,999	
D7 (Military)	6T	1945	1945	Peoria	1,054	
D7C	17A	1955	1959	Peoria	11,708	
RD8	5E8001	1935	1935	Peoria	33	Replaced Diesel Seventy-Five
RD8	1H	1935	1937	Peoria	Incl. below	
D8	1H	1937	1941	Peoria	9,999	Former RD8
D8	8R	1941	1945	Peoria	9,999	
D8	2U	1945	1953	Peoria	23,537	
D8	13A	1953	1955	Peoria	3,703	
D8E	14A	1955	1956	Peoria	3,522	
D8D	15A	1955	1956	Peoria	1,228	Torque converter drive
D9D	18A	1955	1959	Peoria	2,189	Direct drive
D9D	19A	1955	1959	Peoria	1,624	Torque converter drive

TABLE 5: CATERPILLAR PRODUCT LINES—YEAR OF INTRODUCTION

Product	Introduction Year	Models at Introduction	Notes
Crawler Tractors	1925	2-Ton, 5-Ton, 10-Ton, Thirty, Sixty	Merger of Holt and Best
Graders	1928	Motor Patrol No.20	Purchased Russell
Diesel Engines	1931	D9900	
Scrapers (Self-propelled)	1941	DW-10	
Scrapers (Pull-type)	1946	60, 70, 80	
Crawler Loaders	1951	T2, T4, T6, T7, HT4, L2, LW2	Purchased Trackson
Pipelayers	1951	PD4, MD6, MD7, MD8, MDW8	Purchased Trackson
Off-highway Haulers	1962	769	
Wheel Dozers	1963	824, 834	
Wheel Dozers (Tiger)	1997	844, 854G	Purchased Tiger
Forklift Trucks	1965	S-series, P-series	Purchased Towmotor (Incl. Gerlinger lift trucks)
Earth Compactors	1965	824B, 834	
Log Skidders	1971	518	
Excavators (Caterpillar)	1972	225	
Excavators (Eder)	1984	205, 206, 211, 212, 213, 214, 224	Agreement with Eder
Excavators (Mitsubishi)	1987	E70, E110, E120, E140, E180, E240, E300, E450, E650	Joint venture with Mitsubishi
Excavators (Mining)	1992	5130	
Log Loaders/Harvesters (Tanguay)	1985	LL216, LL228, LL229, PL220, FB221, DL221	Agreement with Tanguay
Loader Backhoes	1985	416	
Articulated Trucks	1985	D25C, D30C, D35C, D44, D250B D300B, D350C, D400, D550	Purchased DJB
Rubber-Tire Asphalt Compactors	1985	PS110, PS130, PS180, PS300, PS500, PF200, PF300	Former Raygo products (Raygo purchased 1987)
Single Drum Vibratory Compactors	1985	CS431, CS433, CS551, CS553, CS643 CS653, CP323, CP433, CP553, CP643 CP653, TSF/TSM54. CB521, CB523, CB525	Former Raygo products (Raygo purchased 1987)
Dual Drum Vibratory Compacators	1985	CB214, CB224, CB314, CB414, CB424, CB514, CB614, CB522, CB524, CB624	Former Raygo products (Raygo purchased 1987)
Concrete Finishers	1985	TF250, TC250, TR500	Former CMI products (Reverted to CMI 1987)
Slip Form Pavers	1985	SF175, SF250, SF450, SF500, PS28-300	Former CMI products (Reverted to CMI 1987)
Drum Mix Asphalt Plants	1985	UVM-series, PVM-series, SVM-series	Former CMI products (Reverted to CMI 1987)
Soil Stabilizers	1985	RR250, SS250	Former CMI products
Pavement Profilers	1985	PR75, PR105, PR275, PR450, PR750B PR1000	Former CMI products
Asphalt Pavers	1985	AP200, AP800, AP1200	Former CMI products
Asphalt Pavers (Barber-Greene)	1991	BG220, BG245B, 265B, 750	Purchased Barber-Greene
Agricultural Tractors	1986	Challenger 65	
Underground LHD Loaders	1995	R1500, R1700 II, R2800, R2900	Joint venture with Elphinstone
Telescopic Handlers	1995	TH62, TH63, TH82, TH83, TH103	Former DJI products (U.K.)
Combine Harvesters (Caterpillar)	1925	34, 36, 38	Sold to Deere & Co. 1935
Combine Harvesters (Claas)	1997	Lexion 460, 465, 480, 485	Joint venture with Claas
Skid Steer Loaders	1998	216, 226	

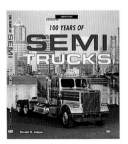
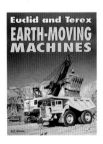

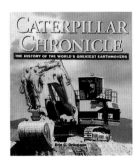